Investing in Children

William U. Chandler

Worldwatch Paper 64
June 1985

Financial support for this paper was provided by the United Nations Fund for Population Activities. Sections of the paper may be reproduced in magazines and newspapers with acknowledgment to Worldwatch Institute.

The views expressed are those of the author and do not necessarily represent those of Worldwatch Institute and its directors, officers, or staff, or of the United Nations Fund for Population Activities.

©Copyright Worldwatch Institute, 1985
Library of Congress Catalog Card Number 85-51252
ISBN 0-916468-64-X

Printed on recycled paper

Table of Contents

Introduction 5
Children of Crisis 8
Primary Concerns 14
Integrated Development 30
Population Growth Versus Health 43
Using the Crisis 53
Notes 57

Introduction

Historian Fernand Braudel describes famine as the "Leader of the dance of Death." Dancing across Africa, it has hit children hardest and threatens to undo decades of progress in improving child health. Its awful figure draws attention to ailing societies and asks what future their children have. Yet, far more children in both Asia and Africa die of malnutrition unrelated to food shortages. Correcting the underlying causes of famine and malnutrition is essential to the future of half the children on the planet.[1]

Child health reflects—and determines—the human condition. It results from and contributes to social development. The growth of societies depends on the capabilities of their people, and these, in turn, depend on health and education. Child health affects growth, learning, and work. Reducing child mortality also reduces parents' economic need to have many children for the work and old-age support they contribute. When mothers have fewer children, they are more productive in agriculture, the fundamental activity of developing societies and one for which women are often most responsible. When child populations are smaller, any agricultural or economic surplus is concentrated on improving fewer minds and bodies.[2] When population and natural resources are more in balance, the environmental effects and economic costs of overpopulation, deforestation, desertification, soil erosion, and water and air pollution are reduced.

Improvements made in child health over the last 20 years stand as an impressive achievement, even in Africa. The notion of a "child survival revolution" has taken root and is spreading.[3] The developing world has cut infant deaths—death during the first year—from 20

I would like to thank my colleague Marion Guyer for assisting with the research for this paper, Norbert Engel, Hans Hurni, Saidi Shomari, and Bassirou Touré for providing access to information, and Engel, Hurni, Judy Jacobsen, and Phyllis Windle for comments on earlier drafts.

percent of live births in 1960 to 12 percent today, though averages mask wide regional variations. Most developing countries even accelerated their progress during the economically difficult decade of the seventies. The World Health Organization (WHO), however, projects that the developing world will not reach the WHO infant mortality goal of 5 percent by the end of the century. Industrial countries, by contrast, have achieved rates between .7 percent and 2 percent. Controversy in the United States over the loss of momentum in reducing infant mortality below 1 percent highlights not only the disparity between rich and poor in that country but the enormous gap between the developed and Third World. The U.S. rate remains relatively high by European standards because infant mortality rates among some minority groups approach 2 percent.[4]

Hunger's victims are always disproportionately children. The horror of famine in Ethiopia has been escalating since 1958, with the infant mortality rate recently reaching 60 percent in some villages.[5] Ethiopia is not alone in its misery. Mozambique, where over 100,000 have died of starvation, continues to face an emergency. Mali, Chad, Sudan, and Niger are among a score of African countries that face severe food shortages. Malawi shows signs of epidemics and increasing mortality. Afghanistan faces famine, and Bangladesh, where diets have been substandard for 20 years, faces a worsening food situation.[6]

These emergencies lead some to openly question the wisdom of helping Third World children survive. They fear that a child survival revolution could push whole populations, even now surviving at the margin, into a Malthusian abyss. Some even question the morality of providing food, antibiotics, inoculations, oral rehydration, and other effective measures against death without also providing tools for agricultural productivity, education, and birth control. Others argue that only economic growth can reduce population growth and provide the resources to care for billions of additional people.

Child survival, it is true, cannot be sustained without fewer births and more food. But the inverse logic, that famine and high infant mortality may be necessary to control population growth, is false. The negative feedback of poor child health to societal growth is just that—negative. Allowing children to die also allows deprivation in sur-

> "More children die because they are improperly weaned than because of famine."

vivors, conditions that retard their, and society's, development. Even in countries that have arguably exceeded their ability to support their populations—Ethiopia, Kenya, Senegal—child death is a burden that not only slows development but impedes efforts to reduce population growth.[7] Because fertility often increases in areas following famine or some other cause of high mortality, these disasters do not regulate population growth.

The notion that economic growth can compensate for and eventually contain population growth has been buried under the weight of recent experience. Throughout Africa and in desperate countries such as Bolivia and Bangladesh, food production and economic wealth are falling further behind population growth. Even with optimistically high economic growth rates of 6 percent, half the world would still earn less than $1,000 per year per capita in the year 2010. This realization prompts the search for other solutions to poverty and ill health. This search necessarily begins with the causes of infant and child mortality.

More children die because they are improperly weaned than because of famine. More children die because their parents do not know how to manage diarrhea than because of epidemics. More children die because their mothers have no wells, hoes, or purchasing power than because of war. They die because their mothers are exhausted from excessive child birth, work, and infection. And when children are stunted and retarded from disease and malnutrition, when overburdened parents cannot generate wealth for education and development, then burgeoning populations inadequately prepared for life add to the degradation of natural systems. These stresses perpetuate drought, disease, and famine.

What is needed today is a strategy of using the crisis, one that meshes the short-term needs of desperate peasant families with the long-term requirements of ecological stability and economic development. The United Nations Children's Fund (UNICEF), noted for promoting child survival measures such as oral rehydration, does just that when it assists women in the Sahel to plant gardens. The village women grow these gardens with water they draw by hand from open wells, one bucket at a time. The gardens yield food for the children. They generate communal income for building a community maternity or school. And they revegetate barren land, providing ground cover to conserve soil, trees that can provide nitrogen and soil nutrients, and microclimate change that, with thousands of other gardens, can help halt the spread of deserts. UNICEF's strategy is often as simple as providing the buckets the women use to draw water.

A child survival revolution requires a development revolution. Warding off death does not ensure a decent life. Primary education is essential for understanding better health and agricultural practices, but, as the relatively literate countries of Tanzania and Bolivia have shown, education will not compensate for lack of incentives in agriculture. Agriculture is the basis of rural economies, but, as India has shown, the "Green Revolution" will not compensate for infected bodies unable to make use of food. Clean water, as many failed projects have shown, will not compensate for a lack of understanding of hygiene. Ensuring child survival will not immediately reduce the perceived need for children. In fact, child survival makes the need for family planning more urgent.

A strategy of integrated development to meet "basic needs" all across the Third World demands not just techniques such as oral rehydration that prevent death, but also policies that promote food production, clean water, education, family planning, and, ultimately, health. It is a strategy that can incorporate measures to counter the drought through revegetation of desiccated lands. It is a strategy of investing in people, one that could truly revolutionize the prospects for child survival.[8]

Children of Crisis

Knowing even the simplest fact of child survival—are fewer children dying?—is not rigorously possible. Data collection, which varies greatly among and within countries, is often supplemented with impressions and vignettes. Some observers claim that numbers are manipulated to suit particular audiences: donors give more funds if the situation is worse, while international health experts are more impressed if the situation is better. Health care for children is a highly

> "Half to two-thirds of child deaths could be prevented with relatively simple measures."

political issue, for in some high mortality countries, foreign aid for health represents a quarter of foreign exchange earnings. Even in China, a country where the need for aid does not skew the data, the rate of infant mortality reported by two United Nations agencies differs by 50 percent.[9]

Analysts generally agree, however, that about 17 million children die each year from the combined effects of poor nutrition, diarrhea, malaria, pneumonia, measles, whooping cough, and tetanus. Virtually all these deaths occur in the Third World. Half to two-thirds could be prevented with relatively simple measures.[10] The cause of death may be ascribed to pneumonia, measles, or malaria, though the "initiating" cause may have been simple diarrhea. To save a child's life from measles may be to lose it to whooping cough. Nevertheless, regional studies and case histories do suggest that the combination of primary education and primary health care has led to rapid progress.

Africa, the continent of crisis, has made great strides toward improving child health. Its nations, however, still dominate the list of those countries with the highest rates of infant and child mortality. (Infant mortality and child mortality are defined as death between birth and age 1, and age 1 and age 5, respectively, expressed in percent.) Only two countries in the Western Hemisphere, Bolivia and Haiti, have very high infant mortality rates—10 percent or greater—while four-fifths of Africa exceeds this level. Africa also compares unfavorably with Asia. Only Afghanistan, Bangladesh, India, Kampuchea, and Pakistan rank as poorly. Their combined populations, however, equal twice that of the high infant mortality African nations. Ironically, the greatest threat in Africa comes from its failure to reduce birth rates in parallel with overall mortality. (See Figure 1.) This is also true for Bangladesh and Pakistan, as well as for most of the Middle East.

China has reduced its national infant mortality rate to a level close to those in some U.S. cities, despite income levels among the lowest in the world. It apparently has already achieved the World Health Organization (WHO) goal for all countries by the year 2000: infant mortality below 5 percent.[11] Food shortages are no longer a serious problem in China, and since the economic reforms that began in 1978, agricultural production has grown 6-8 percent per year, further en-

Rate per
1,000 Population

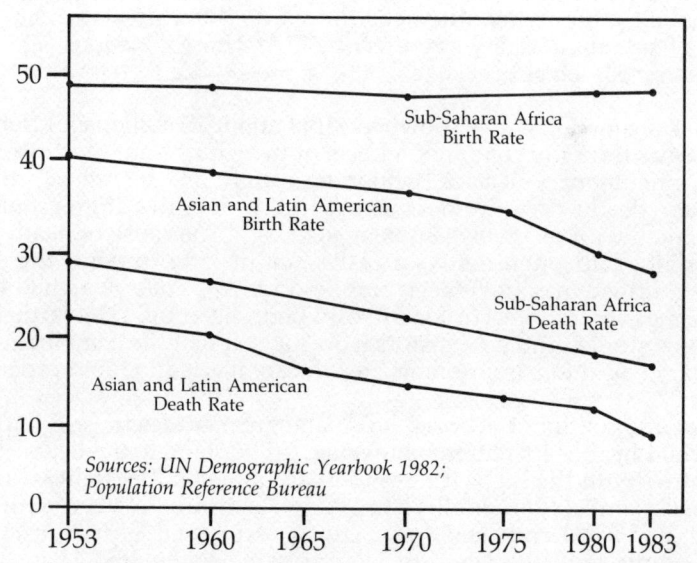

[Chart showing Sub-Saharan Africa Birth Rate (~48-48), Asian and Latin American Birth Rate (declining from ~40 to ~28), Sub-Saharan Africa Death Rate (declining from ~29 to ~17), and Asian and Latin American Death Rate (declining from ~22 to ~9), from 1953 to 1983.]

Sources: UN Demographic Yearbook 1982; Population Reference Bureau

Figure 1: Birth and Death Rates, Selected Regions, 1953-83

suring nutritional sufficiency. China in the last 15 years has achieved the most dramatic, and possibly the most important, reduction in fertility in history.

In Latin America, some countries have cut infant mortality rates impressively since 1960. Mexico has gone from 9 percent to 5 percent, and Brazil from 12 percent to 7 percent. Chile's level of infant mortality has dropped from 11 percent to 2.7 percent in the last 20 years. These countries accelerated rates of improvement after 1972. Improvements may have slowed, however, as economic recession in Latin America reduced per capita incomes by 10 percent between 1980 and 1983.[12]

Low birthweight is a major factor in infant mortality and therefore a useful index of infant health. Incidence of low birthweight around the world fell both in relative and absolute terms between 1979 and 1982, according to rough estimates. In 1982, 20 million babies were born weighing less than 2.5 kilograms, representing about a fifth of all births. Three-fourths of all low birthweight babies are born in Asia, mostly in India, Bangladesh, Pakistan, and Afghanistan. Chinese, Japanese, and South Korean mothers give birth to underweight babies far more rarely than other Asian women.[13]

Rates of malnutrition are another good indicator of overall child health. A crude estimate of global trends in malnutrition in children under age 5 indicates no change in relative terms but a growing malnutrition problem in absolute numbers. (Malnourishment here is defined as below 70 percent body weight for age, using U.S. means.) The number of children malnourished in the sixties and early seventies totaled about 125 million compared to 145 million in the seventies and early eighties. (See Table 1.) Africa experienced an increase of 2 million malnourished children, and Asian malnourished children, excluding China and Japan, increased from 95 million to 115 million.[14] Altogether, an estimated 25 percent of the world's children under age

Table 1: Estimates of Annual Cases of Malnutrition in Children Ages 0-4, by Region[1]

Region	1963-73 (millions)	(percent)	1973-83 (millions)	(percent)
Africa	19.9	31.1	21.9	25.6
Asia	94.8	50.6	114.6	54.0
Latin America	10.8	25.9	8.6	17.7
Total	125.5	26.0	145.1	26.0

[1]The figures are decade averages extrapolated for the regions from country specific surveys. They are approximate and should be used with caution. Asia excludes the Soviet Union, China, and Japan, but includes India, Pakistan, Bangladesh, Burma, Indonesia, Malaysia, Nepal, and other smaller nations.

Source: "Global Trends in Protein-Energy Malnutrition," *Bulletin of the Pan American Health Organization*, Vol. 18, No. 4, 1984.

5 can be described as malnourished. Improvements in Latin America have been offset by deterioration in Asia and Africa, where high birth rates have added to the absolute number of deprived children.

Bangladesh, with 95 million people, has suffered a serious decline in food supply per person since the mid-sixties—even though it was already food deficient then. Between 1963 and 1982, per capita calorie consumption declined 14 percent. Three-fourths of the population now lacks a sufficient diet. Vitamin A intake meets only one-third of requirements. Riboflavin intake meets half of requirements. Yet, possibly because of better hygiene or antibiotics, malnutrition afflicted a lower percentage of children in 1982 than in 1976: 75 percent versus 85 percent. Average height and weight for children under age five increased, although for over-fives, the trend has been negative. Malnutrition is especially acute for women and small children, who more often receive insufficient diets compared with men in many Third World countries.[15]

India, without a reliable census, has begun a semi-annual sampling system to determine health trends. The samples suggest that infant mortality increased from 14 percent in 1971 during the food-short early seventies, and since then has declined to 1971 levels. But independent studies suggest greater improvement and estimate that the infant mortality rate is now about 11 percent.[16]

Even compared with the magnitude of Asia's problems, the situation in Africa appears grim. Decline in infant health is evident even in countries that formerly had made progress. For example, drought has reversed a positive trend in infant mortality in Ghana. Drought-related hunger afflicts 1.1 million in Senegal, nearly half of whom are children. It affects 1.1 million children in Mali and raises the spectre of the drought camps of 1973, where the child mortality rate was 90 percent. Several million could die in Ethiopia, Sudan, and Mozambique.[17]

Countries at war or torn by civil strife, of course, suffer most. In Uganda, which has suffered over a decade of upheaval, only one child in 20 is immunized against the most serious childhood diseases. In regions where fighting continues, the infant mortality rate, 10-12

> "Between 1963 and 1982, per capita calorie consumption in Bangladesh declined 14 percent."

percent nationwide, reaches 14 percent. In Mozambique, antigovernment guerillas have virtually paralyzed transport of relief supplies, and they have viciously attacked schools and murdered health workers. Starving parents, too embarrassed to collect food from distribution camps because they have no clothes, send their children instead.[18]

As fighting creates refugees, it also creates the most acute child health problems in the world. Nine million people worldwide live in refugee camps, with 3.5 million Afghanis, 2 million Palestinians, and 1.2 million Ethiopians leading the list. The camps incubate measles, typhoid, and cholera. In addition, more than 9 million Africans have been uprooted by drought and economic deprivation during the last decade and forced to relocate, often in slums utterly unprepared to handle them.[19]

Health care demands created by food shortages, drought, and war strain the staffs of world relief agencies. Most must focus on the immediate needs of feeding those who might otherwise starve. In terms of grain, the worldwide need for aid totals 10 million tons per year, considerably under the world stockpile. Aid shipments have been generous, but in 1984 half of the 3.6 million tons shipped to Africa went to one country, Egypt, which is not particularly distressed. Aid requirements could, moreover, triple during the next 15 years.[20] And experience everywhere shows that food aid can cause corruption, destroy local markets, and reduce local food production unless managed extremely well.

Many experts caution against famine relief that fails to address fundamental problems. At the beginning of an emergency convoy of food across Mauritania into Mali and Niger, a UNICEF representative wrote, "No operation of this type makes sense unless it is followed by development aid. The African people do not want charity, but support in fighting the disaster themselves."[21] Unless relief is used to help overcome long-term development problems, unless the crisis is used to provide basic needs, long term prospects will not brighten.

The situation of the world's children recalls the question, "Is the glass half full or half empty?" An optimist would answer with the statistic that we have halved the child mortality rate. A pessimist would answer with the figure of famine. A realist would be buoyed by the statistical improvement in child health, but sobered by the fact that, thanks to explosive population growth, as many children suffer and die today as did 20 years ago. Our progress has only offset the growth of our problems.

Primary Concerns

Malnutrition caused by poor child feeding practices claims over 10 times as many children as actual famine. Coupled with diarrheal dehydration, malnutrition is the leading killer in the world, killing 5-8 million children each year, at least 10 percent of all deaths. It is caused by a combination of poor sanitation, infectious diseases such as measles, failure to breastfeed, and poor weaning practices, especially the failure to adequately supplement breastmilk after five or six months of age. The most effective defense against diarrhea, malnutrition, and infections includes nutritional education, breastfeeding, oral rehydration therapy (ORT), and immunization. (See Table 2.) Progress in this

Table 2: Potential Reduction In Infant And Child Deaths With Proven Disease Control Technologies

Cause of Death	Estimated Deaths (millions)	Interventions	Effectiveness (percent)	Potential Lives Saved (millions)
Diarrhea	5	Oral Rehydration	50-75	3
Immunizable diseases	5	Vaccines	80-95	4
Pneumonia/lower respiratory infection	4	Penicillin	50	2
Low birth weight, malnutrition	3	Maternal supplements Antibiotics Contraceptives	30	1
Total	17			10

Source: J.E. Rohde, "Why the Other Half Dies," *Assignment Children*, No. 61-62, 1983.

primary health care strategy can be assessed by measuring progress in each of its components.

Another major component of a strategy to fight malnutrition is female education, both in primary schools and through maternal education. Progress in female education has perhaps contributed most to improving the health of the world's children. Female education is essential in hygiene, oral rehydration, immunization, breastfeeding, family planning—in short, child health. The strongest relationship observed globally in reducing infant mortality is primary school education, even adjusting for better access educated mothers have to sanitation and health care. (See Figure 2 and Table 3.) Countries that have attained both lower fertility and mortality rates also have high female literacy rates. Fortunately, the Third World has made significant progress in literacy. (See Table 4.) In 1960, 28 percent of the world's children did not attend primary school; by 1982, this figure was reduced to 8 percent. The children not in school continue to be found almost exclusively in countries with the highest child mortality rates.[22]

China has shown how much a poor country can achieve with primary education. Currently, 95 percent of its school-age children are enrolled. Primary and pre-school enrollments in China increased about 14 percent between 1983 and 1984. In Hebei province in northern

Table 3: Rate of Child Mortality at Various Levels of Education of Mothers, Nairobi, Kenya, 1979

Years of Education	Child Mortality[1]
	(percent)
None	13.8
1-7	10.4
8 or more	6.1

[1]Percent of children dying by age 2.

Source: W.M. Senga, R. Faruqee, B.A. Ateng, "Population Growth and Agriculture Development in Kenya," Institute for Development Studies, University of Nairobi, Kenya, 1980.

Infant Mortality Rate
(percent)

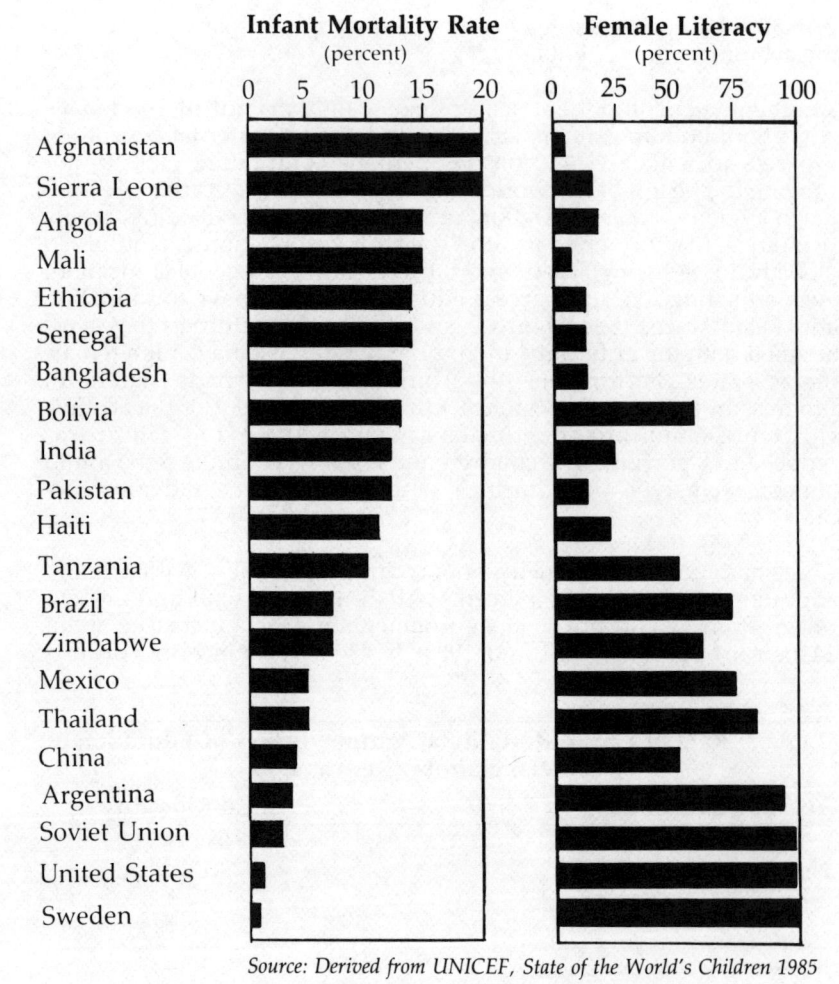

Female Literacy
(percent)

Afghanistan
Sierra Leone
Angola
Mali
Ethiopia
Senegal
Bangladesh
Bolivia
India
Pakistan
Haiti
Tanzania
Brazil
Zimbabwe
Mexico
Thailand
China
Argentina
Soviet Union
United States
Sweden

Source: Derived from UNICEF, State of the World's Children 1985

**Figure 2: Infant Mortality and Female Literacy,
Selected Countries, 1982**

Table 4: Enrollment in Primary School in High Infant Mortality Countries, 1960 and 1982[1]

Country	Boys 1960	Boys 1982	Girls 1960	Girls 1982
	(percent)		(percent)	
Afghanistan	15	54	2	13
Bangladesh	66	76	26	47
Bolivia	78	93	50	78
Ethiopia	11	60	3	33
Haiti	50	74	42	64
India	80	93	40	64
Indonesia	86	106	58	94
Kenya	64	114	30	101
Mozambique	60	102	36	78
Nicaragua	65	101	66	107
Niger	7	29	3	17
Nigeria	46	94	27	70
Pakistan	46	78	13	31
Philippines	98	111	93	108
Senegal	36	58	17	38
Sudan	35	61	14	43
World	85	94	74	83

[1]Percentages over 100 are inflated by age misreporting and pupils over 11 years in first level.

Source: World Bank, *World Bank Development Report 1984* (New York: Oxford University Press, 1984).

China, local officials in 1984 expanded educational opportunities and doubled enrollments in literacy classes by creating more than 5,200 schools. Literacy, through campaigns such as this, has increased among the rural Chinese from 20 percent in the fifties to 80 percent today.[23]

Tanzania has also made noteworthy progress in education, having attained a 70 percent adult literacy rate, the highest in sub-Saharan Africa. Despite Tanzania's ranking among the world's poorest countries, the country's infant mortality rate is half that of the world's unhealthiest countries, though it remains high—10 percent—by industrial nation standards. Food production per capita, however, has declined 12 percent since 1974, and fewer than 2 percent of fertile women practice birth control. President Julius Nyerere concedes that Tanzania has made mistakes, especially in centralizing its government and agriculture. Said Nyerere, "We had useful instruments of participation (local governments and agricultural cooperative unions) and we got rid of them."[24] The Tanzanian experience, along with that of Bolivia, which also has both relatively high literacy and infant mortality rates, shows that although education is a necessary condition for child health, it is not sufficient.

Along with female literacy, nutrition education is an important factor in child health. In most high infant mortality countries, a failure to understand child nutrition is the most serious threat to child welfare. Malnutrition is inextricably tied to disease, sometimes weakening a child's body, making it susceptible to infection, sometimes resulting from disease itself. Most malnutrition is caused not simply by a shortage of food, but by a failure to use food properly. Often parents give children insufficient food—in ignorance—even when adequate supplies are available. In Africa women often breastfeed exclusively for 18 months or longer. Late weaning with poor food is the leading child health problem in Africa. When weaned, many children are given adult foods they cannot chew or digest, or that are unnourishing.[25]

India's child health problems resemble Africa's. A WHO survey found that over 90 percent of Indian mothers breastfeed their children up to one year, and 85 percent still do so after 18 months. Solid food supplements often begin too late, only after 12 to 18 months. Again, weaning practices are the main problem.[26]

Educational campaigns are under way to improve weaning practices in Africa. A poster produced by UNICEF's Ivory Coast office encourages, "After five months, more than the breast."[27] It urges

> "When weaned, many children are given adult foods they cannot chew or digest, or that are unnourishing."

breastfeeding supplementation with, "One food for strength (meat), one for development (fruit), and one for energy (millet/rice)."

Poor nutrition and infection in South America and some parts of Asia increasingly begin with the failure to breastfeed. Bottled milk denies children not only the best nutritional formula, but also antibodies that fight infection. Human milk contains many agents that fight bacteria and viruses. Breastmilk has 3,000 times as much lysozyme—an enzyme that destroys E. coli and some salmonella—as cow's milk. In both urban and rural health centers in northern Santiago, Chile, surveys found that half of all infants were fed breastmilk substitutes by age two months.[28] This rate is similar in Honduras and Venezuela.

The U.N. World Health Organization (WHO) and UNICEF have launched major campaigns to combat the decline of breastfeeding. Beginning with simple education programs through posters and radio broadcasts, efforts now include day-care centers for mothers who work on plantations and in factories. Day-care permits mothers to keep the child close enough to be breastfed, but inflexible work schedules and high costs often undermine such efforts.

Children in high infant mortality countries are often infected by contaminated food and water. During the rainy season, for example, mothers are usually away in the fields for long hours, and they will often leave a pot of porridge for older children to serve to infants during the day. By day's end, bacteria in the unpreserved, unrefrigerated food will have multiplied many times. Worse, food stocks are lowest during the rainy season, when the previous harvest is almost exhausted and before the next is gathered. Exposure to diarrheal disease and malaria are greatest during this time. In the Gambia, half of all late infancy deaths occur during the three-month rainy season.[29]

Malnourished children often have well-nourished parents. Dr. Jean Paul Beau demonstrates this in his rehydration and feeding clinic in the slum of Guediawaye, Senegal. He puts his fingers around the skinny legs of a two-year-old so starved he cannot walk, or even smile. Then, reaching to the child's mother nearby, he pinches the excess fat on her arm indicating that she is not only well-nourished, but overnourished. The mother appears sad and explains, "We never learned how to feed a child." Beau suggests not that the mothers are deliberately depriving their children of food for themselves, but that poor weaning practices and infection cause the malnourishment. The problem often extends to distribution of food within a family. In much of Africa and southern Asia, women are not allowed to eat with men. Men traditionally eat first, and women and children eat whatever is left.[30]

Diarrhea, especially repeated bouts, reduces appetite and is commonly and mistakenly treated by withholding food. The illness also reduces the body's ability to make use of food. Diarrheal infections cause the body to secrete fluids rapidly, and the combined effects of energy deprivation and dehydration are deadly.

Malnutrition frequently involves more than a lack of calories or protein. Severe iodine deficiency, for example, has been discovered along the southern fringe of the Himalayas. Forty million Indians have goiters, and in northern India, 4-15 percent of all newborns have hypothyroid conditions that can impair mental development and motor functions. In the kingdom of Bhutan, one-third of the population of two villages is afflicted with cretinism. Government efforts to iodize salt and to immunize those at highest risk are being undertaken.[31]

Xerophthalmia, or dry eye, continues to afflict 5 million preschool children each year in Asia, blinding 250,000 children each year. The condition, caused by a Vitamin A deficiency, frequently occurs in Bangladesh, India, and Indonesia, as well as parts of Africa and Central and South America. Efforts to control the disease have been led by the Helen Keller International Association, funded by the U.S. Agency for International Development. Techniques include Vitamin A injections, food supplements, and promotion of foods that are high in retinol, the precursor of Vitamin A.[32]

Nutritional failure is evident throughout the Third World, where two-year-olds frequently are reduced to less than 2 kilograms, a figure dangerously low even at birth. One sees them—lethargic, skin inelastic and wrinkled as if aged, buttocks sagging and limbs as thin

> "In much of Africa and southern Asia, men eat first, and women and children eat whatever is left."

as saplings—in their mothers' arms in front of regional clinics. Death is close for such children, but with rehydration and supplemental feeding, they can be revived.

Supplemental feeding programs to alleviate malnutrition can be extremely expensive, but results from recent nutrition research have shown how to make these programs more cost-effective. Various studies show that in supplemental feeding of children, lactating mothers, and pregnant women, concentration on pregnant women has been most effective. One study in the Gambia revealed that vitamin preparations improved the nutritional value of mothers' milk better than more expensive food supplements.[33] Another study from the Gambia found that food supplements to pregnant women did not improve birthweight during the dry season. During the wet season, however, when work is hardest, food in least supply, and the risk of infection highest, food supplements reduced the rate of low birthweight from over 28 percent to less than 5 percent in the study population. This approach is also cheaper because only a small percentage of women will be critically in need of food supplements—only 1.5 percent of women will be in the second half of pregnancy at any given time, even in high birth rate countries.[34]

Reviews of supplemental feeding programs in four countries put the cost of diarrheal death avoided at more than $2,900, even in the best of circumstances. One clinic, Notre Dame du Cap Verte au Pikine in Senegal, however, treats 250-350 patients per day, and the entire operation costs about $2,000 per year. The clinic funds itself by charging 25 cents per person treated. The low cost of the success at Pikine is due to a highly efficient staff, including volunteer work by the mothers themselves. Jean Paul Beau, who works occasionally in this clinic as well as his own, describes the progress of those children saying, "The curves of the corners of their mouths bend into smiles parallel to the curves on their growth charts."[35]

Dehydration, a common factor in malnutrition, is beginning to yield to the elegance of oral rehydration therapy (ORT). ORT consists of a simple sugar and salt solution to correct the ionic imbalance in the small intestine that results from diarrheal infection. The technique averts death in 90 percent of diarrheal dehydration cases. In countries that have adopted ORT, hospital admission rates and mortality from diarrheal dehydration have been cut in half. Only about 10 percent of the children who are at serious risk of diarrheal dehydration ever receive ORT, however. As UNICEF points out, even this low rate already saves a half million young lives each year.[36] ORT is in such demand in the camps of Ethiopia that UNICEF has requested bulk packaging instead of the small, individually-packaged sachets: it is simply too time-consuming to tear them open one package at a time.

Throughout the Third World, health workers are promoting home preparation of ORT mixtures. In the Gambia, Julbrew bottles, which hold beer or soft drinks, are ubiquitous, and health educators have turned them into a tool for child health. They urge a mother whose child has diarrhea to mix eight Julbrew bottle caps full of sugar and one of salt with three bottles of water, and to have the child drink the solution. Elsewhere, posters and radio programs explain how parents can mix a fistful of sugar and a pinch of salt with water to save their children from diarrheal dehydration. Constraints on such efforts can be as simple as a lack of postermaking skills and equipment, and aid agencies frequently contribute this expertise to local health workers.

Controlling infectious childhood diseases has also helped reduce diarrhea-related mortality. For example, diarrhea frequently accompanies measles. Theoretically, vaccinating 75 percent of a child population for measles would reduce diarrheal mortality 10-20 percent.[37]

Only about 40 percent of the world's children, however, have been vaccinated against measles, diphtheria, whooping cough, or tetanus. (See Table 5.) Full coverage against the major childhood infectious diseases would cost only $2-$15 per child worldwide. To extend vaccination coverage to all the world's children would cost an additional $600 million to $4 billion per year.

Particularly effective immunization programs have been conducted by Dr. Jean-Hubert Thieffry of the Enfant de Partage organization in the Thies Region of Senegal. Health care workers visit remote sites in mobile units that permit quick travel from village to village. All across Thies one sees long lines of mothers waiting to have their children

> "Only 40 percent of the world's children have been vaccinated."

Table 5: Global Immunization Rates For Infectious Diseases, 1980

Disease/Inoculation	Children Vaccinated (percent)
Diphtheria, Pertussis, Tetanus[1]	41
Measles	37
Polio	43
Tuberculosis	54

[1]Combined inoculation; pertussis is known commonly as whooping cough.

Source: Derived from UNICEF, *State of the World's Children 1984* (New York: Oxford University Press, 1984).

inoculated against polio, measles, whooping cough, tetanus, diphtheria, yellow fever, and tuberculosis.

A major problem with immunization campaigns everywhere is the dropout rate for the second and third in the usual series of inoculations. Dropouts are due to the inconvenience of returning for more shots, as well as fears stimulated by the minor fevers and aches experienced by children after the first shot. Thieffry reduced his dropout rate by shortening the series of shots from three to two. Some say that combining antigens in only two inoculations reduces their effectiveness. But Thieffry's detailed analysis discounts this concern. Since his teams were created in 1981, they have attained an 80 percent coverage rate for the first shot and almost 60 percent for the second. In 1984, no epidemics of measles or whooping cough occurred in the region served, nor were there any cases of polio or tetanus.[38]

Participation in immunization programs is encouraged by good advance work. The Thies team visits village leaders six months before the planned date of arrival in a village. If they consent to participate, the team arrives again the day before scheduled inoculations to announce their availability. The next morning the mothers and children gather and the workers explain that they have a choice between risking the effects of a "little disease"—the fever and aches that sometimes follow vaccination—or the "big disease"—the all too familiar results of polio, for example. The mothers are put at ease and made to feel comfortable about returning with their children for the second series of shots. The mobile team workers, wielding pneumatic guns in each hand to inoculate two buttocks at a time, effectively immunize villages of several hundred in a morning.

Brazil has successfully conducted mass immunization campaigns, declaring the second Saturday in June and the third Saturday in August as "National Vaccination Days." The government promotes the campaign through loudspeakers and thousands of radio advertisements. Eighteen million Brazilian children have been immunized in this campaign, leading to some dramatic results. Polio cases, for example, dropped from over 2,500 in 1979 to 10 in 1983. Colombia also launched a massive campaign based on the National Vaccination Day concept. It includes endorsement by the country's president, and mobilization of the Red Cross, police, military, United Nations agencies, and tens of thousands of volunteers to supply and deliver vaccines. In a few months, three-fourths of the child population was vaccinated. El Salvador, during a lull in its civil war, sent out immunization teams in a similar effort to vaccinate 400,000 children. National campaigns are encouraging because in some countries, such as rural areas of Mexico, mobile teams have not achieved high coverage rates.[39]

India began extended immunizations in 1978 with a goal of vaccinating all two-year-olds by 1990 for six diseases. Progress has been noticeable, with diphtheria-pertussis-tetanus (DPT) inoculations increasing from 6 million in 1981 to 10.3 million in 1983. Polio vaccinations increased over the same period from 1.3 to 4.4 million. Vaccination against tuberculosis increased from 13 million to 14 million. Unfortunately, the dropout rate between the first and the third doses of DPT and polio is 30 percent. More unhappily, the annual number of newly eligible children totals more than 24 million.[40]

One Nigerian clinic has improved the efficiency of immunization services and attained higher rates of inoculation without increased costs. The clinic had been taking detailed case histories because staff members feared that inoculating children with recent illnesses could cause dangerous reactions. But the recordkeeping imposed heavy

> "Mobile workers can immunize villages of several hundred in a morning."

workloads on the staff and created long waits for mothers and children. This cautious practice had reduced immunization coverage elsewhere, in Sri Lanka, for example, by 70 percent. The Nigerian clinic decided to take less detailed histories, and so far has seen no serious reactions. Meanwhile, DPT coverage in the area served by the Nigerian clinic increased by 8 percent within 6 months, and oral polio vaccine coverage improved by 60 percent. Completed immunizations of infants rose to 18 percent. Waiting time for mothers was cut by an average of one hour, an important consideration for working women. Staff workload was also reduced.[41]

Breakdown in the cold chain, the series of refrigerators needed to store and transport vaccines, frequently interferes with inoculation efforts. The problem is more than technical, involving corruption and favoritism in the delivery of vaccines. The U.S. Centers for Disease Control has urged international health agencies to slow their efforts to expand immunizations in some areas, fearing that people's expectations will become too high. This is particularly likely where programs cannot be adequately monitored.

No country can afford to promote ORT, nutrition education, and immunizations as separate items. Primary health care must be delivered as a package. The effectiveness of the entire package determines long-run success or failure. Many large-scale primary health care efforts in India, Indonesia, and the Philippines have failed to reduce infant mortality.[42] Most suffered from poor supervision of health workers.

An example of a relatively successful program in West Africa suggests both the potential and the problems with primary health care. In the Gambia, village health workers are trained for six weeks, then provided with simple tools of the trade: oral rehydration salts, antibiotics, bandages, anti-malarial drugs, aspirin, and other curative items that villagers badly want. They learn to recognize diarrhea, measles, whooping cough, malaria, or cholera. Workers teach mothers to administer the ORT salts for episodes of diarrhea, and not to wait until the child is dehydrated. They make a record of such cases on picture-sheets, usable by illiterates, and then follow-up the initial contact with a home visit. Workers ensure that advice is followed and explain how to prevent recurrence of diarrhea or other avoidable problems. Difficult cases are referred to a district health post staffed by more highly trained workers, or to a regional hospital, which the parents can reach within a day's travel by donkey cart, and where a doctor is available.[43]

Supervisors with two years of training monitor the work of five village health workers. Supervisors visit each village once weekly to ensure that drugs are available, records are kept, and preventive services are performed. If special problems arise, regional medical professionals are alerted. This system enables the health ministry to respond quickly to any epidemic of measles or cholera, and to dispatch an emergency team to give immunizations or to take other preventive actions, such as securing the water supply. Malaria incidence has also been reduced in children by dispensing chloroquine, an effective anti-malarial drug, to feverish children during the rainy season, particularly when their resistance is low due to depleted food stocks from the previous harvest.[44]

A similar but separate network of maternity workers has been developed. Workers selected by village committees or traditional birth attendants are given several weeks of training to ensure that they practice sterile delivery, monitor maternal weight gain, and provide nutritional counseling. Each worker gets a simple tool kit: an apron, forceps, and drugs to stop hemorrhaging. They are instructed to refer very young, old, or other high-risk women to the regional clinics.[45]

A vast difference in performance, however, can be seen even within this tiny country. A random inspection of villages in the central region reveals that some village health and maternity workers fail to live up to expectations. Records are not kept. Children with eye infections, measles, or injuries are in evidence. The maternity kits appear poorly maintained or unused. Sterile razor blades are not replaced when the original supply runs out. Here infant mortality approaches 17 percent—the national average—and maternal mortality is over 1 percent. In the nearby Arasemmi district, using almost the same approach, infant mortality is only 5 percent. Better administration, and perhaps more positive tribal attitudes toward hygiene, account for the difference.[46]

> "In the Gambia, diphtheria, tetanus, and whooping cough affected less than 1 percent of all patients in 1984."

Administrative problems have been relatively easy to identify. Poor recordkeeping is due to lack of training. Administrators acknowledge that 6-8 weeks is not enough time to convince people who have never kept written information that it can be useful to distant strangers. Inadequate training is blamed on shortages of funds and a rush to meet international goals and guidelines. New workers, health organizers say, would benefit from longer training. For workers already practicing, intensive retraining is attempted each year.

The absence of formal recordkeeping, however, does not guarantee that the system will fail. Weekly visits to each village by health supervisors have created an oral network that enables the national center to quickly respond to epidemics. In the Gambia, measles, diphtheria, tetanus, and whooping cough together affected less than 1 percent of all patients visiting clinics in 1984. Though primary health care has a long way to go in the Gambia, absence of epidemics in that country indicates that the system is working.[47]

The importance of building a foundation for health care has been shown in China. The Chinese system of "barefoot" doctors is a classic example of what can be done to improve the human condition with a minimum of resources. Since the fifties, these rural health workers have spent most of their time delivering simple curative care. They also act as preventive technicians, inspecting water and sanitary systems and providing health education. By providing curative services that the villagers want badly, health workers gain leverage in delivering preventive services.[48]

The system's success is substantiated by China's relatively low infant mortality rate. Also, China probably could not have achieved its low population growth rate without its primary care system. The benefits of recent economic reforms in China, however, have come with negative side effects. Barefoot doctors were previously supported by mandatory insurance fees collected from farmers belonging to the state-run communes. Now that 80 percent of the communes have been replaced by private farming, the central government no longer dominates health care. Responsibility is left to the Chinese counties, which cannot match the revenues from mandatory insurance fees. Many peasants now use fee-for-service doctors, many of whom formerly worked as barefoot doctors. Other people use their new wealth to bypass the local barefoot doctor and seek care in a regional center or hospital. A bout of hepatitis treated in a hospital, however, can cost $160, the annual disposable income of a typical Chinese peasant. William C. Hsiao of the Harvard School of Public Health cites these changes as an argument for mandatory national health insurance.[49]

Thailand, which has reduced infant mortality from 10 percent to 5 percent since 1960, represents another success story. The country further upgraded primary care in 1977, and by 1979, the government had trained six thousand health workers. Most of these were "health communicators" with only two days training. Nearly a thousand were village health workers given two weeks training, and almost a hundred were nurses who received additional training of one year. Nurses were assigned to health centers serving five thousand people each. As in China, family planning services are delivered through the primary health care system. Thailand has cut its population growth rate from 2.9 percent in 1960 to 1.9 percent in 1985.[50]

India's government-sponsored primary health care system has "flopped completely," according to one assessment, though the verdict is the opposite for voluntary programs.[51] The difference between them seems to be not in philosophy or approach, but in supervision and administration. Private health care personnel are more motivated by incentives and feedback. An interesting exception to this situation is in the state of Kerala, where, despite low incomes, female literacy is high, primary health care is progressing, and infant mortality is less than half the national average.

A primary health care project established in Guatemala among the Cakchiquel Indians in 1962 has thrived and is now expanding into other kinds of development projects. Land tenure, for example, seriously constrains economic and health development in the highlands where the Indians live. In response, the health project established a revolving loan program for peasants to buy land. Water well projects and female education, including information on the value and methods of child spacing, have also been established. For the poorest people, health care is provided on credit.[52]

> "In Nepal, girls under age five are twice as likely to be undernourished as boys."

Kenya has invested heavily in primary health care since independence in the sixties, with considerable success. A pre-independence infant mortality rate of 12.6 percent has been cut to 8.3 percent. But a recent weakening in the national economy has hampered primary health care efforts. The usual shortages of drugs, fuel, and spare parts have been reported. Compounding the problem is the spread of malaria strains resistant to chloroquine, the principal malaria-fighting drug.[53]

Worldwide experience with primary health care suggests that local funding is required. Without fee-for-service, central governments cannot sustain salaries, supplies, and service. The conversion of the Sine-Saloum primary health care system in Senegal from near collapse to reasonable efficiency is a case in point. Eliminating duplicate services, reinforcing supervision and training, and instituting fee-for-service helped save the program.[54]

Discrimination against females throughout the Third World extends to health care. Surveys in rural Karnataka, India, showed that men receive health services at a rate three times higher than women. Women's services are oriented to mothers and ignore the needs of women who are not pregnant or lactating. Moreover, 80 percent of the community's health workers are men. In neighboring Nepal, girls under age five are twice as likely to be undernourished as boys, and xerophthalmic blindness, caused by chronic malnutrition, is twice as likely to strike women as men.[55] Combating this situation requires development efforts targeted at women. Education helps remove superstitions behind the abuse of women and provides the basis for improving both the lives of women and primitive economies.

The record in primary health care is mixed. Most developing countries practice some level of primary care, and countries such as China, Thailand, Costa Rica, and Sri Lanka have had considerable success. Others, such as Colombia and Brazil, have impressive immunization programs. UNICEF and WHO have spurred the global movement to promote breastfeeding where its practice is decreasing. And oral rehydration, vaccines, antibiotics, and progress in female education have, over the last 20 years, cut the rate of worldwide infant mortality almost in half. This achievement is unprecedented in history. Sadly, the progress has been diminished by drought and the growth of human numbers. The world has not invested enough in primary care, population planning, or social and economic development to reduce the absolute numbers of people suffering. Relative improvements are satisfying only to the fortunate whose children do not suffer and die.

Integrated Development

"Ndokh," said the Senegalese woman, speaking the word for water in her native Wolof. Stressing each letter, she added, "It is my only problem." Her assertion was remarkable given her circumstances: annual income less than $400; seven children; a drought that had cut her harvest in half; a firewood shortage that requires her to spend hours each week searching for wood. But with her vegetables, watered from a 30-meter hand-dug well, one bucket at a time, she feeds her family. During the worst drought of the century in the Sahel, she and her female colleagues have created a large green garden on parched and barren earth.[56]

Across the Sahel one sees this new phenomenon: women's cooperative gardens. Sometimes organized by an "animatrice," usually a young college-trained African, they more often are begun by the women themselves who decide that something must be done. The hardest part is finding water. Without abundant water supplies, progress in hygiene and agriculture is impossible. Before UNICEF assisted some gardens in Senegal, in fact, the women did not even have enough buckets to hand-irrigate the fields.[57]

Every country with high infant mortality shares similar shortcomings in basic development. Primary education, health care, clean drinking water, water for hygiene, and tools for food production are lacking or nonexistent. A fundamental cause of high infant mortality in Africa, the Middle East, and southwest Asia—the high infant mortality bloc—is a lack of training, funds, and materials to provide these services, as well as a failure to target women as the essential providers of them. Like the Wolof woman, the Nepalese, Bengali, or Bolivian women lack fuel, sufficient food, and the tools to produce more of either. Projects that provide simple tools, such as buckets for

> "The northern third of Senegal now lies almost barren."

gardens, loans for fertilizer, and wells for drinking water and improved hygiene, directly redress these problems of underdevelopment.

La Sécheresse, as the West Africans call the drought that has plagued them for 20 years, adds another dimension to underdevelopment, eroding even the barest levels of subsistence. Mauritania has been virtually overtaken by the Sahara. The northern third of Senegal, formerly a typical Sahelian savannah, now lies almost barren. In Dakar, the sky is filled with dust for most of the year as the Harmattan wind peels off topsoil in the northeast and carries it hundreds of kilometers southwest. Mauritanians and Senegalese move from the north to the slums of Dakar, or even farther south to Guinea-Bissau. With them go hundreds of cattle that strip vegetation in their path.[58]

The Sahelian drought has devastated the women and children who live there. In one survey of Mauritania, 45-55 percent of the children had experienced diarrhea within the past two weeks, and 12-17 percent were below average in weight-for-height measurements. Food aid was erratic and minimum nutritional requirements were unmet, particularly of vitamins A and C. Maternal mortality was high, though experts only guessed the figure.[59]

Water plays two important roles in this malnutrition crisis: its shortage reduces not only food production, but also food use efficiency. Contaminated wells, buckets, and pots, along with unpreserved food, carry diarrheal disease into children. When women walk up to three hours to get minimal water supplies, water becomes too valuable for washing, and an important defense against infection is lost. The association between water and health is second only to that of female education and child health. (See Figure 3.) The strength of this relationship and the direct bearing water wells now have on garden crop production and community development have led UNICEF to dedicate a quarter of its global budget to providing simple water supplies. In Ethiopia, after relief, water is the largest item in the UNICEF budget.

Infant Mortality Rate
(percent)

Access to Clean Water
(percent)

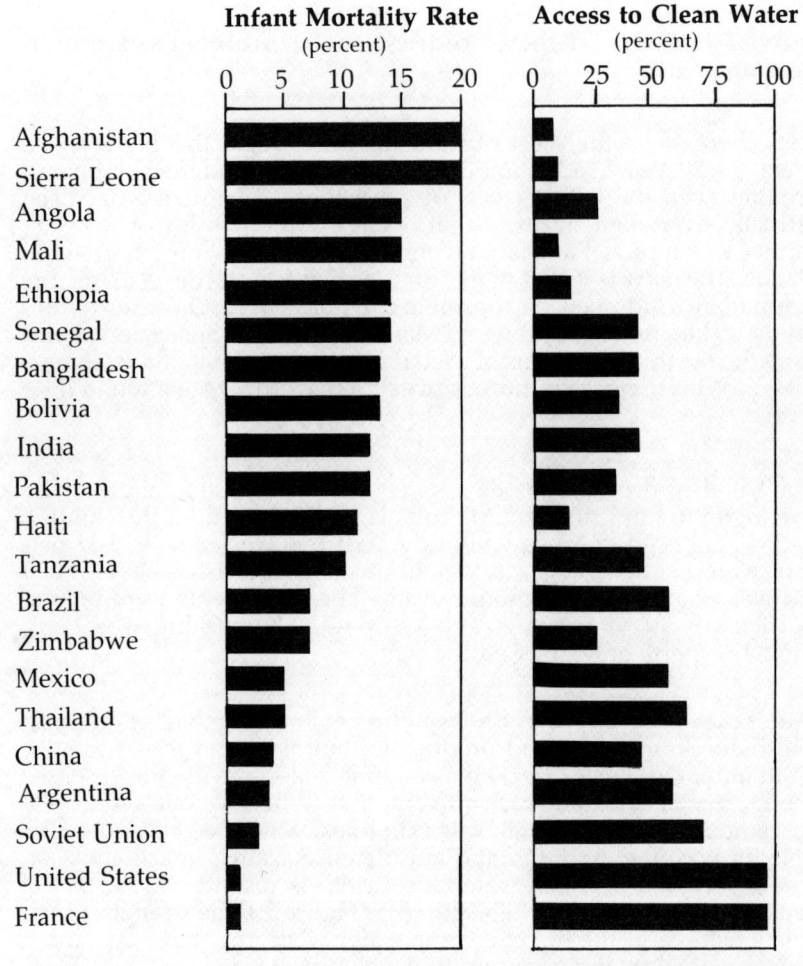

Afghanistan
Sierra Leone
Angola
Mali
Ethiopia
Senegal
Bangladesh
Bolivia
India
Pakistan
Haiti
Tanzania
Brazil
Zimbabwe
Mexico
Thailand
China
Argentina
Soviet Union
United States
France

Source: Derived from UNICEF, State of the World's Children 1984.

Figure 3: Infant Mortality and Share of Population with Access to Clean Drinking Water, Selected Countries, 1982

Even where available, most wells are open to contamination. Often animals are watered from the same wells as drinking water is drawn. Without a concrete apron, bacterially contaminated water will seep into the well. Piped and chlorinated water is generally unaffordable in the high-mortality countries, but sealing and protecting wells, even in village settings, can be made affordable.

The water bucket is a major source of contamination. Held in dirty hands or placed on filthy ground, it can easily spoil a well. The bucket and pulley ropes can be sealed to prevent soiling, though this requires some expense and expertise. Well placement also requires expertise. If placed in a depression, it can be easily contaminated. If too shallow, it will dry up near the end of the dry season. Hand-dug wells usually dry out fastest because they are shallow: digging far below the water table requires expensive hydraulic equipment.[60]

Because water contaminated with feces or urine is a major source of disease, toilets are essential. Diarrhea and roundworm each affect more than a half billion people, and clean water and rudimentary sanitation could eliminate almost half of these cases. Ninety percent of all cholera cases could be prevented with adequate sanitation systems. Their design and placement can be complicated, however, and costs are sometimes high. Toilets must provide privacy, not contaminate groundwater, and last 10 years. Screened vents are required to remove odors that will deter use. Pit latrines meeting these requirements can be installed for less than $10 per user in the Third World.[61]

Many water and sanitation problems are behavioral rather than technical. But some technologies are not appropriate for rural use. If a pump has many moving parts and is complicated or expensive to fix, the first time it fails will be the last time it is used. Similarly, if toilets do not control flies they will be abandoned.

Zimbabwe has long funded a unique institution to develop solutions to such problems. The Blair Research Laboratory has, since 1939, developed controls for malaria and schistosomiasis, and designed systems for clean water and sanitation. The Blair Toilet, the prototype vented pit latrine, and the Blair Pump have become internationally renowned for their effectiveness and low cost. The pump is a shallow well pump, completely sealed and sanitary, with only three moving parts. It has no handle or lever to break. It consists simply of two pipes, one of which moves inside the other, and two one-way valves. The pipes are plastic and can break, but these can be repaired in five minutes with glue by someone who has an hour of training. Thirty thousand Blair Pumps and 20,000 Blair Toilets have been installed in Zimbabwe since 1981. The laboratory promotes this effort not only with demonstrations, but with simple educational materials.[62]

Although controlling water-borne bacteria will reduce malnutrition, it will not reduce under-nutrition caused by food shortages. If food production in southern Africa, for example, grows only at historic rates of 1.4 percent per year while population continues to grow at 2.2 percent per year, the region can expect what the U.N. Food and Agriculture Organization (FAO) describes as a "doomsday trend." Southern Africa has not been self-sufficient in food since the sixties, and only the most optimistic agricultural forecasts foresee self-sufficiency before the year 2000. Cereal imports, in fact, are expected to multiply eightfold by the year 2000 and cost $4 billion per year in foreign exchange. The FAO estimates that Angola, Mozambique, Botswana, Zambia, and Tanzania will fall short of the investment capital needed to become food self-sufficient by a total of more than $2 billion per year. The prospect that southern Africa will be unable to continue food imports to meet future demands is, according to the FAO, "too grave to contemplate." [63]

East and West Africa face a similar scenario, as does much of southern Asia. Twelve of Afghanistan's 28 provinces are threatened by famine, partly as a result of war. A half million people are at risk of starvation.[64] Bangladesh, described as a "basket case" in the early seventies by Henry Kissinger, still suffers severe malnutrition in three-quarters of its children. India, by contrast, has moved from food deficits to secure stocks, and even exports some grain. The difference in India is that food aid in the sixties was used to force agricultural reforms that encouraged peasants to grow a surplus. India was also helped by advances in agricultural technology that became known as the "Green Revolution."

Index
(1961-65 = 100)

Source: U.S. Department of Agriculture Data
Note: China's index based on 1955-65.

China

Latin America

Bangladesh

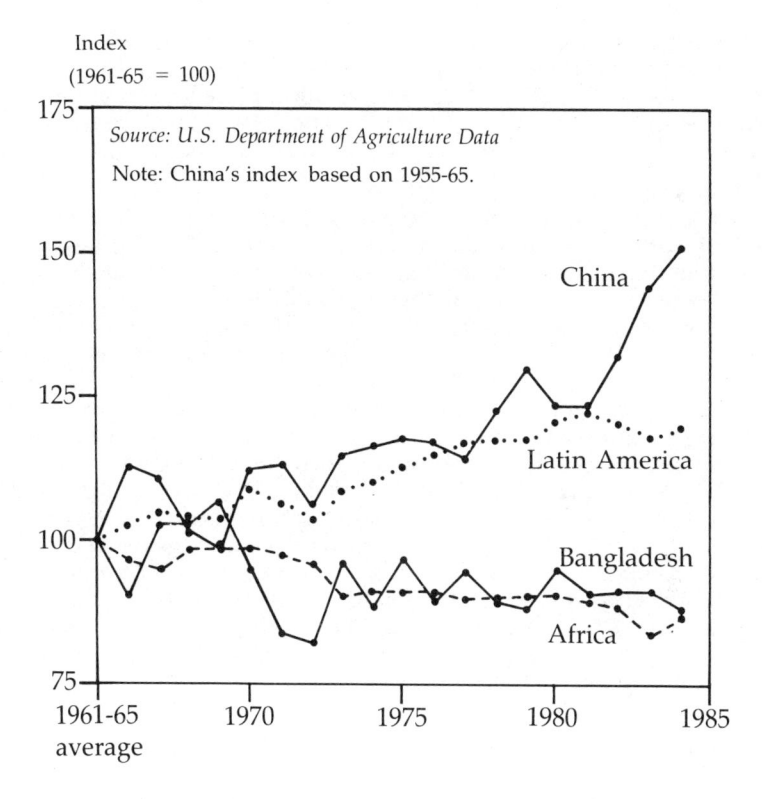

Africa

Figure 4: Food Production Per Capita, Selected Areas, 1965-84

Food intake per person in Bangladesh has fallen since the early sixties, a fact that can be attributed to falling food production per capita. (See Figure 4.) Grain production has increased only 1 percent per year since 1965, compared to a 2.8 percent population growth rate. Farmers lack seed, irrigation during the dry season, means to control erosion, and access to capital to improve production. Moreover, prices for food products are controlled to protect the urban middle class. Analysts suggest remedies that parallel those for Africa: small hand wells for irrigation, local reforestation projects, loans for farmers without collateral, and better incentives and markets for farmers.[65]

China has demonstrated the power of agricultural reform. In 1984 China had a record grain harvest and became self-sufficient in grain for the first time in the modern era. Its impressive recent agricultural gains have come not from state investment, but from market incentives, especially the opportunity for peasants to sell food surpluses on their own. Throughout Africa, however, agricultural policy stymies production. An exception is Zimbabwe, which five years ago ended a decade of war over land distribution and apartheid. The new Zimbabwe government, under Prime Minister Robert Mugabe, maintained incentive pricing for commercial crops and preserved the capital and skills of the established farmers while promoting peasant agriculture. Land operated by resident commercial farmers was not expropriated, but land owned by absentee landlords was redistributed to peasants. More important, peasant farmers received loans of about $600 each. The result was that peasants, aided by the end of drought in southern Africa, produced enough food in 1985 to feed the country, leaving commercial farm output for exports to earn badly needed foreign exchange.[66]

Agricultural pricing reforms can greatly increase production. A World Bank analysis of price distortions in agriculture, foreign exchange, and manufacturing showed an inverse relationship between price controls and economic growth in 31 Third World countries. Countries ranking low in price distortions, including Thailand, South Korea, Cameroon, and Malaysia, had rates of growth averaging over 6 percent during the seventies. Countries ranking high in price distortions, including Tanzania, Chile, Bangladesh, and Nigeria, experienced low rates of growth. Making the transition between a highly regulated economy and one free of price controls is difficult, as many countries—including Sudan most recently—have discovered. But China, again, has shown that a staged withdrawal from price distortions can be managed.[67]

> "One-third of the cultivated land in southern Africa could be irrigated by small projects."

Agricultural reforms are among the most important steps needed to relieve famine in Africa. But the famine has many causes, and action will be needed on many fronts. Caste systems, bad weather, environmental degradation, war, and overpopulation all contribute to the crisis. Some relief agencies have recognized the need to integrate food, water, and relief efforts. The Permanent Inter-State Committee for Drought Control in the Sahel (CILSS), for example, recently announced a $2.3 billion multi-year relief effort with one-fourth of the funds allocated for food assistance and over one-third for groundwater supplies. The project also includes dune stabilization, forest planting for fuelwood and soil protection, integrated development of forest and agricultural areas, small-scale forest industries, and forest management.[68]

A similar integrated effort has been recommended for southern Africa by the United Nations. Plentiful supplies of groundwater, generally shallow, make small-scale irrigation possible for about $500-$1000 per hectare, less than one-tenth the cost of large-scale irrigation and within the means of traditional farmers, if financing is provided. Eleven million hectares, about one-third of the cultivated land in southern Africa, could be irrigated by small projects. Additional financing will be required to increase fertilizer use four- to fivefold, and to fight a dozen pests and diseases that combine to reduce harvests up to 40 percent. Agricultural extension services will be needed to offer assistance in managing livestock, which now overgraze land by more than 50 percent in some areas.[69]

Particularly troublesome in improving the productivity of peasants—in agriculture, water supply, or household crafts—is access to financing. Peasants often have no direct ownership of communal land or land of sufficient value as collateral for loans. Women have even less access, for they usually do not hold title to land that their families might own. One development organization, the International Fund for Agricultural Development (IFAD), provides loans to such persons by offering a simple incentive: failure to repay means further loans are denied. Often the loans are given to a group, and so peer pressure is placed on individuals whose failure to repay would jeopardize the entire group. The IFAD has a 95 percent repayment rate, but only $1 billion in loan funds. Even that may be lost due to donor country budget-cutting.[70] To service all of peasant families in Africa and south Asia who do not have access to financing would require a fund of $40-$75 billion.

Women must receive much higher priority in water, health, and agricultural development. Women do over half the work involved in food production in non-Muslim parts of India and in Nepal, and up to 80 percent in Africa. (See Figure 5.) Yet, extension agents, loans, fertilizer subsidies, and most other productivity improvement projects are aimed at men. But with simple devices that can be produced

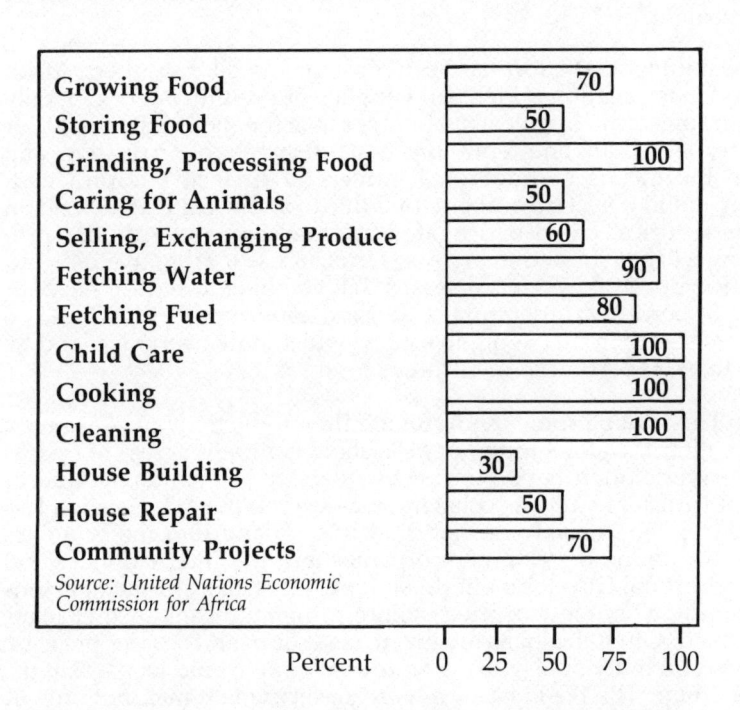

	Percent
Growing Food	70
Storing Food	50
Grinding, Processing Food	100
Caring for Animals	50
Selling, Exchanging Produce	60
Fetching Water	90
Fetching Fuel	80
Child Care	100
Cooking	100
Cleaning	100
House Building	30
House Repair	50
Community Projects	70

Source: United Nations Economic Commission for Africa

Figure 5: Share of Work Performed by Women in Africa

locally, such as hoes, buckets, fertilizer, and efficient wood stoves, women's workloads can be eased and some buying power generated, particularly if they control the marketing of their products.[71]

Some women have found a way to improve their situation. They persuade their husbands to dig several open wells, erect a fence, and prepare the soil, and they do the rest. They plant tomatoes, lettuce, beans, bananas, and other fruits. The gardeners usually keep half the money from their individual plots and give half to a community fund. Some groups have built new maternities and schools, and with some help, have equipped and operated them.

Communal garden projects are an ideal target for development assistance. They provide women with not only food but also increased economic power, which usually means increased status and decision-making authority. Improved agriculture also means a better environment and a long-term reduction of the deforestation that worsens drought. One African leader, whether facing the reality of women's work or continuing the bias against men doing such work, has a slogan, "one woman, one tree." Though the original Chinese version, "one person, one tree" is preferable, it is a start. As garden projects become more successful, men may take over the marketing of the produce, reducing benefits to women. To prevent this, several development agencies have organized women's market cooperatives.

Any development project must account for how work will be divided according to traditional norms. A project in Kenya, for example, increased agricultural productivity, but also increased the time women spent on food production by a third. Men shared a smaller part of the burden because they usually do not help in food harvesting and storage. Additional tools for harvesting or a shift in the division of labor could be contrived for such occurrences.

The importance of integrating development with conservation projects is readily apparent. In West Africa, members of the Wolof tribe have a riddle that explains how the countryside was once in ecological balance, enabling the local population to withstand drought. It asks, "Where does the dry season go in rainy season, and where does the rainy season go in dry season?" The answer, "Into the acacia tree."[72] The acacia is a nitrogen fixing tree, with leaves in dry season, and none in wet, that when growing in Sahelian fields increases some yields 80-300 percent. A development program that gives buckets for watering gardens to those who plant trees acts two ways. It integrates the short-term motivation of women, who want to feed their children, with the long-term need to revegetate vast areas of the Third World, especially the Sahel. If women can be persuaded to plant acacias to improve their gardens—perhaps paid in the form of fertilizer or additional tools—then their yields will increase in a few years and their children will enjoy a habitable climate in the future.

Family planning has been successfully integrated with development of women's agriculture. The Indonesian National Family Planning Coordinating Board (BKKBN) established a program called "Beyond Family Planning," providing loans of $500-$5,000 to women's groups when at least 55 percent of their members practice family planning. The program not only reduces the "acceptor" dropout rate, but attracts many women who might otherwise not participate. Almost 60 percent of Indonesia's eligible couples now practice family planning, and the country has a goal of a 93 percent acceptance rate by 1990. "Beyond Family Planning," started with the help of the United Nations Fund for Population Activities (UNFPA), was expanded by the BKKBN, and is now supplemented by private banks because the repayment rate has been high.[73]

Where famine relief is needed, a timely opportunity exists to use short-term aid to solve long-term problems. Nowhere has this been more dramatically demonstrated than in Ethiopia. In response to food shortages, the government and the UN World Food Program began distributing food in return for work. Many people object that starving people cannot work, but the object is to prevent starvation, not simply avert it temporarily. Food for work projects began because Ethiopians suffering famine will remain in their villages until it becomes unbearable. Then they leave in search of a road, city, or camp to find food. By that time, it is virtually too late. Many have lost 30 percent of their body weight, and children may be beyond help. Often children are left behind by the parents seeking food, who are then unable to return because of forced resettlement or sickness.[74]

> "Ethiopians, working for food with hoes and shovels, have built 600,000 kilometers of terraces for controlling soil erosion."

An alternative is to distribute food before the villagers become wasted and abandon their homes. Ethiopians, for example, working with hoes and shovels, have built 600,000 kilometers of terraces for controlling soil erosion. They have planted 500 million tree seedlings. Swiss soil conservation scientist Hans Hurni is using food for work to initiate soil and water conservation. The projects will avert famine in the short term by providing grain, and help solve a basic cause of famine in the long term: soil degradation and climatic change.[75] These efforts, if sustained for 20 years, can help reverse the ecological decline in Ethiopia.

Food for work, or even cash for work programs, have succeeded elsewhere. UNICEF has used the latter approach with Ethiopians who built protected water supplies or irrigation ditches using the many springs found in the highlands. Peasants used cash payments to buy food, averting famine often caused more by a lack of purchasing power than from absolute food shortages. Food for work projects have begun across the Sahel in efforts to plant gardens, reforest the desert, and create micro-climate changes. The approach will not work everywhere. Nomads, for example, will not usually remain behind to sustain efforts. But progress in Ethiopia has been substantial, largely because of the social organization and cooperation made possible by Peasant Associations, cooperatives organized by the government and composed of all the farmers cultivating an area of 800 hectares.[76]

Failures in food for work projects, however, are all too familiar. In Bangladesh, food aid possibly does more harm than good for the intended beneficiaries. Food relief shipments flood markets and depress the earnings of poor farmers while merely reducing food costs for middle class city-dwellers. Throughout the Third World, corruption and incompetence in distribution of food are common. But most forms of development assistance suffer these problems. Rather than abandoning food for work, such programs should be more carefully monitored. They will need careful planning, also, to avoid compounding existing problems. Digging a well for human water supply, for example, can attract herders with their cattle and thus accelerate devegetation.

Land shortages pose serious constraints in most of the Third World. In Bangladesh, population growth and political inequality have left 45 percent of the peasants landless. This problem grows in proportion to population, which is increasing at a rate of 2.8 percent per year. Landlessness will become more common in Pakistan, India, and throughout Africa as population pressures increase. In southern Africa, where land is relatively plentiful, farmland can be expanded only by a third. Yet, population is expected to double before stabilizing.[77]

Boosting agricultural production greatly depends on appropriate government policy. Farmers must get a fair price for their crops, and, in the long run, that can only occur with market pricing. Sometimes price supports and commodity programs are necessary to break the cycle of subsistence agriculture, for if a peasant must sell at harvest time to pay taxes or school fees, he might earn much less than if crops can be stored until markets improve. The United States' agricultural system was boosted in part due to cash loans to farmers for grain placed in reserve. If prices went up, the farmer could sell and receive higher earnings, though part of the profit would go to the government-sponsored commodity program. If prices fell, the government would assume most of the loss. This type of risk-sharing program would ease the transition from subsistence to commercial agriculture in the poorest countries. Commercial markets and money economies are necessary if peasants are ever going to accumulate more than just enough food to last until—or almost until—the next harvest.

Integrated development at a scale sufficient to arrest declining living conditions, though relatively expensive, will be affordable. Water and sanitation projects to provide safe water supplies within ten years to the third of the world's population that lacks them would cost about $10 billion per year. Extending loans of $250-$500 to some 150 million Third World peasant families for farm improvements would require an initial loan fund of $40-$75 billion. Interest costs, however, would total only about $7.5 billion annually, and most of this could be recovered. Much of these funds will have to come from the developing countries themselves, but development assistance, appropriately designed, can provide a large boost.

Investing in peasant agriculture to increase productivity and reduce environmental damage is worthwhile in its own right. Productivity improvements are usually large and provide rapid payback. Loans to peasants without collateral can be made relatively risk-free to the lender. And when the funds for investment come from bi-lateral or multi-lateral sources, they can be tied to agricultural reform. But most important, investment in agriculture is also a good investment in children. For without a sound agricultural base, societies will be unable to grapple with overpopulation and economic decline, and malnutrition, poverty, and even famine will spread.

Population Growth Versus Health

Rapid population growth in the world's poorest countries recalls the myth of Erisichthon. In this ancient Greek legend, Erisichthon was cursed with becoming hungrier the more he ate. Poor families are caught in a similar trap: they need many children to help with the work and provide security to parents in old age. But by having more children, families share fewer hectares of land, fewer liters of water, and less income per person. The only escape from this trap is having fewer—but more productive—children. Family planning improves the lives of children two ways: by increasing health care and educational services available per child; and by making more likely the survival of an individual child.

Family planning has the greatest impact on infant mortality when it is used to prevent high-risk pregnancies. These include pregnancies to mothers under age 20 and over age 35, pregnancies spaced close together, and pregnancies after a mother has already had several children. Families that minimize high-risk pregnancies lose fewer children and so do not need one or two extra as "insurance," to ensure that the desired number of children survive.

The risk of infant death is high for very young mothers, whose bodies may not have matured enough to deliver a healthy child. (See Figure 6.) Princeton researchers James Trussell and Anne Pebley point out that family planning is unlikely to reduce early pregnancy unless girls marry later in life. Age at first marriage varies across Africa, generally

Infant Mortality
(per 1000 births)

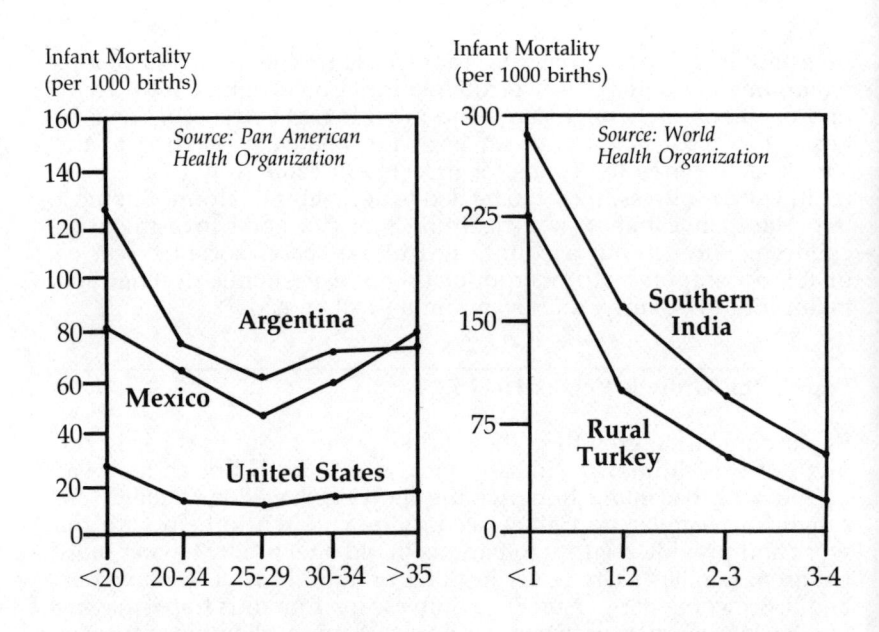

160—
140—   Source: Pan American
       Health Organization
120—
100—
80—   Argentina
60— Mexico
40—
20—   United States
0—
  <20 20-24 25-29 30-34 >35

**Figure 6: Infant Mortality
and Age of Mother**

Infant Mortality
(per 1000 births)

300—
              Source: World
225—   Health Organization

                    Southern
150—   India

75—   Rural
           Turkey
0—
   <1   1-2   2-3   3-4

**Figure 7: Infant Mortality
and Years Between Births**

being lower in the West and higher in the East. In Guinea and Niger, for example, most women marry before age 17. In Senegal, Mauritania, Mali, Nigeria, and Chad, most females marry before age 18. Age at first marriage in Kenya has increased from 18.5 years to over 20 between 1962 and 1979, but birth rates have increased anyway. Bangladeshi women, on the average, marry before age 16, though Asians in general marry later than Africans. Most South American women now delay marriage until age 20 or later. Sixteen years is the minimum age for marriage for women in many developing countries, though in many African nations, girls may legally marry at age twelve.[78]

The length of time between births—child spacing—is crucial at all ages. A child's chances of survival are reduced by pregnancies in

Infant Mortality
(per 1000 births)

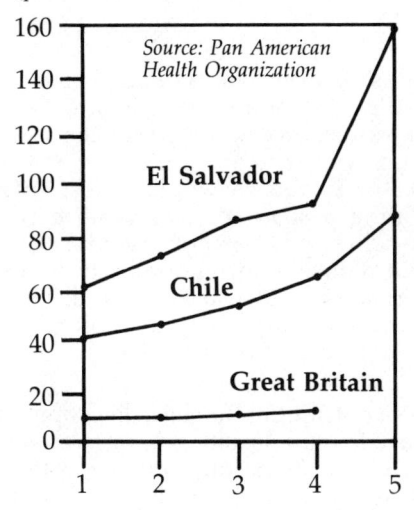

Source: Pan American Health Organization

Figure 8: Infant Mortality and Birth Order

rapid succession that deplete a mother's nutritional reserves and overall condition. Children born close together also compete for maternal care and resources. The previously born child will be at higher risk because breastfeeding is likely to be withdrawn sooner. (See Figure 7.)

Early cessation of breastfeeding can, at the same time, shorten birth intervals. Breastfeeding stimulates the production of hormones in women that reduce ovulation and the risk of pregnancy. This evolved as a natural mechanism to protect the health of both mother and child. Areas where breastfeeding is declining, in fact, experience the shortest birth intervals. In a survey of 26 countries, 30 percent of births were spaced fewer than 24 months apart. Intervals are longer in Africa, because the traditions of breastfeeding and post-partum abstinence—which frequently exceeds one year—are still practiced. But in all of the 26 developing countries surveyed, at least 15 percent of births were inadequately spaced.[79]

An infant's chances of survival also depend greatly on the number of children delivered by the mother. (See Figure 8.) Maternal depletion and competition for resources account for the risk. One study using World Fertility Survey data suggests that family planning for mothers between the ages of 20 and 34 would reduce infant mortality by 5 percent. Maintaining a space of two years between births would reduce infant mortality by 11 percent. Avoiding more than four births per mother would reduce infant mortality by about 8 percent. Child and maternal mortality would also be reduced. The cumulative reductions, though obviously large, are difficult to estimate, however, because of the complexity of their interplay.[80]

Family planning's contribution to child development is also crucial at the social level, where high fertility gets translated into reduced living standards. Primary education, nutrition, and water and sanitation are essential to child survival and development, but rapid population growth can overload a society's ability to provide classrooms and food. The educational disadvantage of growing up in a developing country is large and growing. The World Bank estimates that Western countries spend 50 times as much per primary school student as do the least-developed countries. Yet, the school-age population of a country such as Kenya will almost double by the year 2000. If such countries act to rapidly reduce population growth, the cost of educating their children can be cut in half over the next 25 years. Savings can be used to improve the quality of education, reducing the immense gap in education between rich and poor lands.[81]

Nutrition in poor countries can also decline with population growth. Population growth in Africa, the fastest in the world, has outstripped food production increases by 20 percent over the last two decades. Sluggish agricultural production contributed to this shortfall, but Africa's population grew so fast that food demand could not have been satisfied, even if Africa's farmers had performed as well as south Asia's. China, which both reduced population growth and greatly

> "Maintaining a space of two years between births would reduce infant mortality significantly."

increased agricultural production, now uses its agricultural surplus to generate a higher standard of living. (See Table 6.) The chance that countries such as Ethiopia and Bangladesh can follow China's example, however, is becoming increasingly remote. These countries face a 20-40 percent decline in arable land availability per person in the next 20 years due to population growth, even under optimistic scenarios for family planning.[82]

The elements of family planning are well understood, but questions remain on how to promote and deliver it. Early marriage and childbearing in the Third World are inextricably tied to the economic and social rewards that societies attach to childbearing. Without improvements in the status of women, increased economic security for families, and food supplies less dependent on child labor, family planning cannot fully succeed. But without effective family planning, efforts to improve the quality of life cannot succeed.

Changes in social attitudes toward family planning in the Third World usually reflect government leadership. Most population policy analysts describe progressive government policy as the biggest factor in rapid fertility decline. African nations have been far more reluctant to support family planning than the rest of the world, and they are paying the price. Nevertheless, Africa's leaders have shown a growing awareness that population growth plays a serious role in reducing

Table 6: Average Annual Growth in Population and Food Production, Selected Areas, 1965-85

Region	Population	Food Production	Per Capita Food Production
	(percent)	(percent)	(percent)
China	1.8	3.9	+ 1.1
South Asia	2.0	2.4	+ .4
Africa	2.7	1.8	− .9
United States	.7	1.2	+ .5

Source: Derived from U.S. Department of Agriculture data.

economic growth and living standards. The impetus for family planning efforts in the Gambia, Kenya, and Zimbabwe, for example, has come from ministries of finance, where budget officers projecting future revenue needs become alarmed when they see where current rates of population growth are leading. Assessing recent abrupt changes in attitude, Nancy Harris of International Family Planning Assistance observes that "Africa has made 30 years of progress in family planning in the last five years."[83]

The new awareness of African leaders is typified in a recent speech by President Kountche of Niger:

> It is established...that our rate of demographic growth is not at all in step with our economic growth rate. In other words, our tendency to create needs is vastly superior to our capacity to produce the corresponding vital resources....How [can we] reconcile demographic growth and economic growth taking into account, of course, the sacrosanct regulations of Islam and the traditional values which we have inherited? How [can we] free our society from the socio-educational sluggishness, from fatalism, apathy and running away from responsibility which are obstacles to its maturity and equilibrium?
>
> Is it normal to impose on a woman successive pregnancies which impair the life of the mother and that of the child? Is it normal to inflict on our sisters in the towns and particularly in the country the almost inevitable obligations to become old before their time, crushed under the weight of daily work and ravaged by almost constant nursing?...We should guarantee the future of our children.[84]

Such awareness is vital for bringing Africa's population growth into harmony with its resources. If Africa had the financial power of Europe or Japan and the agricultural and technical resources of the United States, it could, perhaps, support a quadrupling of population. Additional mouths could be fed by increasing grain production per hectare, now only a quarter that of Europe and the United

> "Africa has made 30 years of progress in family planning in the last five years."

States. But no such miracle is in sight: Africa, realistically, must cope with peasant agriculture and modest incomes for the forseeable future, as must India, Pakistan, Bangladesh, and many other Third World countries. If government leaders recognize this fact and incorporate it into their national planning, family planning can succeed.

Family planning success requires that governments set the stage for acceptance. A government's ability to forecast demographic and economic trends plays an important part. Governments influence fertility through laws on minimum age at marriage, statements on the need for and acceptability of contraception, and promotion of birth control devices. Governments can provide training for family planning workers, integrate family planning with primary health care services, and offer incentives or disincentives for having children. By keeping records and evaluating family planning programs, governments provide feedback to help ensure success. The United Nations Fund for Population Activities (UNFPA) supports governments in these efforts with demographic surveys and population projections.[85]

A recent study by scientists Robert Latham and Parker Mauldin ranked family planning programs around the world and found striking regional differences. China scored highest among developing countries, followed by countries in Southeast Asia and Latin America. As a region, the Middle East and Africa ranked last. In terms of a percentage of the maximum score, sub-Saharan Africa scored only 14 percent compared with 70 percent for Southeast Asia. These scores are reflected in fertility, which has not declined in Africa for decades. Eighteen countries, however, have since 1965 reduced fertility by at least 25 percent, including Brazil, China, Colombia, Indonesia, Thailand, and Turkey. Another 16 countries experienced 10-25 percent reductions, including Egypt, India, Mexico, the Philippines, and Vietnam. The use of contraception also reflects these scores, though it lags behind recent improvements in national programs. Only one country in sub-Saharan Africa, Kenya, rated a relatively high score. A strong national family planning policy, or lack of it, was the most important variable in how well countries scored in the survey.[86]

Many nations with low family planning scores are Muslim. Afghanistan, Pakistan, Bangladesh, and many countries of West Africa, for example, rank lowest in family planning. Polygamy and a preference for sons seriously complicate family planning in Islamic countries. Some wives compete to have the largest number of male children. But important exceptions such as Indonesia, where fertility dropped 28 percent during the seventies, and Tunisia, which has the highest average age of first marriage of any Arab country, show that family planning can succeed despite religious impediments. Similarly, many Catholics in both the developed and Third World use contraceptives, despite Vatican opposition.[87]

Since 1965, China has reduced fertility from 7.5 to 2.3 children per woman. Its success is often considered unique, a product of its culture and government. But China's approach includes economic incentives that can work in a variety of cultures. Families with only one child receive benefits, including better access to education and health care, while families with two or more children are penalized. A parallel policy of increasing the status of women, beginning with the enrollment of 90 percent of all girls in school, may in the long run be just as important. Traditional Asian preference for sons, based on economics, may have led to the revival of female infanticide, although this practice has a long history and cannot be blamed on the one-child family policy. Increased education and expanded job opportunities for females make them more valued by parents. More than any Third World country, China has tried to improve the status of women. Females in China now have a longer life expectancy—a measure that should reflect the extent of infanticide—than any other poor country, averaging 69 years. Improving sexual equality will pay many dividends, for it contributes not just to the success of family planning but to economic growth and the quality of life in China.[88]

A preference for sons in many societies presents enormous difficulties for family planning. American Museum of Natural History anthropologists Stanley and Ruth Freed summarize the problem:

> "One eye is no eyes and one son is no sons," runs a popular [Indian] saying....The vast majority of Indians have no social security, private pension plans, or annuities; they rely instead on their sons. Few couples are satisfied with just one son, for the rate of infant mor-

> "The average travel time to a family planning outlet in Thailand is only eight minutes."

tality, while steadily declining, is still high enough to make parents with only one son very anxious....People try to have two or three sons, hoping that one of them will survive to care for them in their old age.[89]

Such attitudes are strong arguments for improving child health. More certain that their children—their social security—will survive, parents will find it advantageous to have fewer children.

Thailand has demonstrated the importance of the availability of family planning services. Thailand, like China, also achieved a dramatic reduction in birth rates during the seventies, when fertility fell almost 40 percent. The Thai government created a National Family Planning Program in 1970 and sponsored services in contraception and sterilization. Among rural women, four out of five depend on government services for contraception, and no one has to travel more than an hour to obtain birth control devices. The average travel time to a government outlet, in fact, is only eight minutes. Studies of the Thailand experience reveal that contraception availability is self-reinforcing. Supply seems to create its own demand.[90]

A group called "Concerned Women for Family Planning" has made a special effort to overcome the extreme constraints imposed by "Purdah" on women in Bangladesh. Purdah is the practice of secluding women, not just behind veils, but in the confines of the home. Women under such tyranny obviously have difficulty obtaining family planning services, or even knowing about them. To counter these conditions, five women in Dhaka have organized services on a door-to-door basis. The group's members are well received by the target women, though they experience resistance from mothers-in-law and husbands. The group overcomes this resistance with follow-up meetings to explain the benefits of practices such as child spacing. They hand out pills and condoms donated by international family planning groups, and return to their clients' homes to provide check-ups. The group, still voluntary, has grown to 4,000 members throughout Bangladesh. It now serves 80,000 women, 70 percent of whom practice family planning, and hopes to serve more in the future.[91]

Although Tanzania has made two decades of progress in improving female literacy and providing primary health care, only 1 percent of the Tanzanian women of childbearing age practice contraception. One reason may be the extremely low access to and availability of contraceptive devices. Though contraceptives could be supplied through an extensive primary health care system, they are not, because birth control is not a priority.[92]

Kenya presents a special example of the situation in Africa. Usually, modernization brings on a slowdown in the population growth rate of a nation. Access to education for females, work outside the home, and reduced infant mortality in Kenya have not brought expected reductions in fertility rates. Only 7 percent of the country's women of childbearing age practice contraception, and most do not plan to begin doing so soon. The average fertility rate is 8.1 children per woman. Moreover, most women want many children—seven on average. Relatively low infant mortality combined with low rates of family planning have given Kenya one of the highest population growth rates in world history, over 4 percent per year. Reversing this growth must begin by filling demand for family planning, which averages 10 percent of fertile women.[93]

Providing family planning services would not be unduly costly. According to Joseph Speidel of the Washington-based Population Crisis Committee, family planning services for a Third World couple cost about $10 a year. For about $4 billion per year, according to Speidel, the world could provide family planning to all Third World families who want it. About $500 million is currently being provided by international donors, plus $1.5 billion spent by developing countries themselves, including $1 billion spent in China. Speidel estimates that family planning programs over the last 15 years have reduced world population by 130 million, saving $175 billion in food, shelter, clothing, health care, and education.[94]

If family planning is essential for improving the health of societies, it is absolutely vital to improving the status of women. In many lands, women are regarded practically as beasts of burden, or second class citizens at best, a condition as unjust as any in human history, including slavery. Girls often are expected to marry soon after menstruation

> "Malawi experienced 8 percent annual economic growth throughout the seventies, yet still ranks fourth worst in the world in child health."

and begin producing children. "It is the duty of a wife to have children," say Indian villagers, and the wife is expected to derive little pleasure from the marriage arrangement. In Zimbabwe, it is said that a woman should bear one child for every cow her husband paid for her when they were married.[95]

The common goals of improving human nutrition, health, physical wellbeing, and the status of women all require greater efforts in family planning. The achievements of China, Thailand, and Indonesia demonstrate that these goals can be reached. Though family planning has come under recent attack, the burden of proof is on critics to show how human needs in Africa and Asia can be satisfied without rapid and permanent declines in population growth.

Using the Crisis

The African famine has alerted the world to at least some of the people living on the edge between subsistence and dissolution. But disaster threatens millions more in parts of Asia and Central and South America. A third of the world's people live in countries where most people are illiterate, a third of the children are malnourished, and children die as often as adults. Any assessment of a child survival revolution must also ask, "Survival for what?" The answer is that children need development as well as survival to help make their lives more than a series of crises.

Failed development efforts, however, litter the landscape with abandoned factories and silted reservoirs. Most development aid assumes that economic growth alone will improve health, nutrition, and education. This kind of development, modeled after the successful Marshall Plan following World War II, relies on foreign aid, reduced domestic consumption, and increased savings to stimulate economic growth. A country like Malawi, however, experienced 8 percent annual economic growth throughout the seventies and yet still ranks fourth worst in the world in child health. After many examples such as this, it has become obvious that rapid economic growth will not necessarily improve living conditions for the majority of people in developing countries.[96]

An alternative development strategy focuses on improving education and health and resists foreign investment, particularly from the West. Tanzania, for example, worked hard to increase literacy and improve child health. Economically, however, Tanzania and many countries following this model stagnated because they eliminated incentives for agricultural and industrial production and cut themselves off from badly needed foreign capital.

China has recently shown how these two development strategies can be effectively combined. The country made necessary investments in population quality, as measured by low infant mortality and high literacy rates, but these alone did not stimulate economic growth. Now that incentives for private agricultural production have been introduced, large gains are being made. China, the model for developing countries in primary health care and primary education, has now become the model for economic development as well. It is proving right economists such as Nobel laureate Theodore Schultz, who argues that investment in people is far more important than investment in machines. China is also proving that market pricing and financial incentives are powerful forces for improving economic conditions. If adopted throughout the Third World, the Chinese triad of primary health care, primary education, and agricultural reform could spur a lasting child survival and development revolution.

Extending primary health care and clean water and sanitation to the world's poorest people, numbering some 1.5 billion, would cost an additional $35-$50 billion per year. This cost includes an extra $4 billion per year for family planning, without which all such investments will be in vain. Extending primary education to the 100 million children who do not now receive it would cost perhaps $5 billion annually. Extending loans for agricultural productivity to some 150 million subsistence farmers would cost $5-$10 billion per year, assuming a revolving fund of about $50-$75 billion, repaid mostly from productivity increases in peasant agriculture.[97] The magnitude of this incremental sum, roughly $65 billion, is not large in relative terms. It would total one-eighth of the economic product of the target countries, and only one-half of 1 percent of world economic output. It does, however, total twice the world's annual provision of development aid.

> "Disasters will only grow
> unless investments are made
> in family planning, health care, and education."

The world's poorest people themselves can hardly increase their savings to provide the funds for development. Consumption can be reduced further only with difficulty. Much waste and corruption exist in the Third World, but without outside pressure—which can be exerted with aid—reform is unlikely. Additional funds will have to come from the developed world. The United States, which in absolute terms is the world's largest aid donor, gives less in terms of percent of GNP than all but 2 of the 17 nations of the Organisation for Economic Cooperation and Development (OECD). Eastern Bloc countries give 30 percent less than the United States in terms of donations as a percent of GNP. Only about 45 percent of currently donated funds are spent on health, education, and agriculture. Some 30 percent are spent on energy projects and public utilities, projects that rarely aid the world's poorest. Much of the world's official emergency aid to African famine victims has simply been reallocated from existing programs.[98]

If such investments—investments in the next generation—make so much sense, why have not more been made? The reasons vary, but they include the fact that savings necessary for investment have been wasted by both natural and man-made disasters. Investments in children also do not pay off for a long time, and most people have far more immediate needs. People in the Third World are not unwilling to sacrifice for their children, but their margin of existence is so narrow that they often must choose between their children and their own lives. The poor health of women in so much of the Third World reflects just this choice.

In these cases developed countries can siphon off part of their surplus to help out those where no surplus exists. An outpouring of private donations to famine victims suggests that people feel compelled to provide disaster relief. But disasters will only grow unless investments are made in family planning, health care, and education, and so will the costs of disaster relief. When development relief does more than just stave off famine, when it is invested to provide benefits for years to come, then savings—in lives and money—will be made. Growth in the Third World means additional prosperity in the developed world through increased trade. But a burden also rests on those who could have helped so many at so little cost, but did not.

Notes

1. Fernand Braudel, *Civilization and Capitalism, 15th-18th Century: The Structures of Everyday Life* (New York: Harper and Row, 1981). For a discussion of investing in human population quality, see Theodore Schultz, *Investing in People* (Berkeley, Calif.: University of California Press, 1981).

2. Kathleen Newland, *Infant Mortality and the Health of Societies* (Washington, D.C.: Worldwatch Institute, March 1981). For an excellent analysis of the effect of population growth on economic development, see World Bank, *World Development Report 1984* (New York: Oxford University Press, 1984).

3. United Nations Children's Fund (UNICEF), *State of the World's Children 1985* (New York: Oxford University Press, December 1984).

4. *World Bank Atlas 1985* (Washington, D.C.: The World Bank, 1985); *State of the World's Children 1984* (New York: Oxford University Press, 1983); "The Major Public Health Killers," *International Health*, Magazine of the International Drinking Water and Sanitation Decade, Oct.-Nov.-Dec., 1984.

5. Mesfin Wolde Mariam, *Rural Vulnerability to Famine in Ethiopia: 1958-1977* (New Delhi: Vikas Publishing House for Addis Ababa University, 1984).

6. Institute of Nutrition and Food Science, "Nutrition Survey of Rural Bangladesh," *ADAB News*, Association of Development Agencies in Bangladesh, May-June 1984.

7. World Bank, *World Development Report 1984*. This report defines carrying capacity for these nations and describes how they have exceeded it.

8. Paul Streeten et al., *First Things First: Meeting Basic Human Needs in the Developing Countries* (New York: Oxford University Press, 1981); Theodore Schultz, *Investing in People*.

9. *World Development Report 1984; State of the World's Children 1985*.

10. For a discussion of this potential, see William U. Chandler, *Improving World Health: A Least Cost Strategy* (Washington, D.C.: Worldwatch Institute, 1984).

11. Adopted by the Thirty-fourth World Health Assembly in 1981; see also *Development of Indicators for Monitoring Progress Towards Health For All by the Year 2000* (Geneva: World Health Organization, 1981); UNICEF, *State of the World's Children 1984* (New York: Oxford University Press, 1983).

12. *Ibid.* See also UNICEF's discussion of the effects of the recession on child health in *State of the World's Children 1984.*

13. "Worldwide Incidence of Low Birthweight," *Bulletin of The Pan American Health Organization,* Vol. 18, No. 3, 1984.

14. "Global Trends in Protein-Energy Malnutrition," *Bulletin of The Pan American Health Organization,* Vol. 18, No. 4, 1984. Although weight for height is a more reliable index of malnutrition, the only available worldwide data for long time periods are in terms of weight for age.

15. M. Chaudhuri, "Malnutrition of Rural Children and the Sex Bias," *Economic and Political Weekly,* August 25, 1984.

16. S. Preston and P. Mari Bhat, "New Evidence of Fertility and Mortality Trends in India," *Population and Development Review,* Vol. 10, No. 3, 1984.

17. Conference on the Emergency Situation in Africa, March 11, 1985, Geneva, "Report on the Emergency Situation in Africa," United Nations, February 22, 1985; "Africa: The Land Is Growing Old: What Will The Children Inherit?," *UNICEF NEWS,* Issue 120, 1984; Lindsey Hilsum, "Mozambique Emergency," UNICEF, Nairobi, undated; "For Mali, groundwater reserves may be only hope," *Christian Science Monitor,* March 25, 1985.

18. "Insurgency adds to Mozambique's problems," *New York Times,* November 25, 1984; Lindsey Hilsum, UNICEF, Nairobi, Kenya, private communication, March 1985.

19. "Slow Recovery in Uganda," *The Lancet,* July 14, 1984; "World opens doors more slowly to millions of refugees," *Christian Science Monitor,* November 16, 1984; "Report on the Emergency Situation in Africa."

20. "Famine in the age of plenty," *South,* February 1985.

21. Deborah MacKenzie, "Suicide in the desert," *New Scientist,* November 29, 1984.

22. Derived from *State of the World's Children 1984.* A simple regression of infant mortality on female literacy in 130 countries yields a correlation coefficient of .75.

23. "Educators say 3 million learned to read in 1984," *China Daily,* February 27, 1985; "Literacy increases within rural areas," *China Daily,* February 9, 1985.

24. "Nyerere resignation to end 23-year era in East Africa," *Washington Post*, December 9, 1984.

25. Margaret Cameron and Yngve Hofvander, *Manual on Feeding Infants and Young Children* (New York: Oxford University Press, 1984).

26. "Food program for pregnant women raises infant birth weight, gestational age, reduces mortality," *Family Planning Perspectives*, Vol. 17, No. 1, 1985.

27. Poster displayed at UNICEF office in Dakar, Senegal, March 1985.

28. J. Welsh and J. May, "Anti-infective properties of breast milk," *Journal of Pediatrics*, Vol. 94, No. 1, 1979; I. Bravo et al., "Breast-feeding, Weight Gains, Diarrhea, and Malnutrition in the First Year of Life," *Bulletin of the Pan American Health Organization*, Vol. 18, No. 2, 1984.

29. Norbert Engel, UNICEF Information Officer, Dakar, Senegal, private communication, May 4, 1985.

30. "Diarrhoea, dehydration, and drugs," *British Medical Journal*, November 10, 1985; *State of the World's Children 1984*; Jean Paul Beau, L'Organisation de Science et Technologie d'Outre Mer, Pikine, Senegal, private communication, March 6, 1985.

31. "Extreme iodine deficiency in India is believed to disable millions," *New York Times*, April 2, 1985.

32. "Vitamin A Deficiency: Signs, Symptoms, and Solutions," *Horizons*, Winter 1985.

33. Andrew Prentice et al., "Dietary Supplementation of Lactating Gambian Women," *Human Nutrition: Clinical Nutrition*, No. 37C, 1983.

34. Andrew Prentice et al., "Prenatal Dietary Supplementation of African Women and Birth-weight," *The Lancet*, March 5, 1983; R. Feachem, "Interventions for the control of diarrhoeal diseases among young children: supplemental feeding programmes," *Bulletin of the World Health Organization*, Vol. 61, No. 6, 1983.

35. Sister Samuela Beeizza-Disperiraine, Notre Dame du Cap Verte, Senegal, private communication, March 6, 1985; Jean Paul Beau, personal communication, March 6, 1985.

36. *State of the World's Children 1985.*

37. R. Feachem and M. Koblinsky, "Interventions for the control of diarrhoeal diseases among young children: measles immunization," *Bulletin of the World Health Organization,* Vol. 61, No. 4, 1983.

38. Jean-Hubert Thieffry, "Une These de Medicine," Université d'Anies; Michelle Thieffry, Voluntaire du cooperation, Thies, Senegal, private communication, March 1985.

39. "One way to get results," *World Development Forum,* October 15, 1984; "Vaccination blitz," *China Daily,* February 5, 1985.

40. R. N. Basu, "India's immunization programme," *World Health Forum,* Vol. 6, 1985; "1985 World Population Data Sheet," Population Reference Bureau, Washington D.C., 1985.

41. Ebun Ekunwe, "Expanding immunization coverage through improved clinic procedures," *World Health Forum,* Vol. 5, No. 4, 1984.

42. W. Henry Mosely and Lincoln Chen, eds., *Child Survival: Strategies for Research,* reprinted in *Population and Development Review,* Supplement to Vol. 10, 1984.

43. Hattib N-Jie, Deputy Director, Medical and Health Ministry, the Gambia, private communication, March 12, 1985.

44. *Ibid.*

45. Bertha M-Bodge, Director, Maternal and Child Health Services, Medical and Health Ministry, the Gambia, private communication, March 14, 1985; Norbert Engel, UNICEF Information Officer, Dakar, Senegal, private communication, March 14, 1985.

46. Norbert Engel, private communication, March 15, 1985.

47. Curt Fischer, Regional Medical Director, Medical and Health Ministry, The Gambia, private communication, March 16, 1985. Data on recent reductions in mortality in epidemics from Norbert Engel, private communication; Hattib N-Jie, private communication.

48. *China: The Health Sector* (Washington, D.C.: World Bank, 1984).

49. William Hsiao, "Transformation of Health Care in China," *New England Journal of Medicine,* April 5, 1985.

50. *State of the World's Children 1984.*

51. R. N. Basu, "India's Immunization Program."

52. Carroll Behrhorst, "Health in the Guatemalan Highlands," *World Health Forum,* Vol. 5, No. 4, 1984.

53. Sheila Rule, "Kenya's rural clinics face increasing strain," *New York Times,* February 3, 1985.

54. Margaret Palato and Michael Favin, *Primary Health Care: Progress and Problems* (Washington, D.C.: American Public Health Association, August 1982); Abby L. Bloom, "Prospects for Primary Health Care in Africa," *A.I.D. Evaluation Special Study No. 20,* U.S. Agency for International Development, Washington, D.C., April 1984.

55. "Nutrition and energy expenditure of poor women," *AP-Tech Newsletter,* October 1984; "Women and children last," *Women in Development,* December 1984.

56. Oumy Ngoné and Thiam Diofyor, Departement Funela, Senegal, private communication, March 3, 1985, translated by Bassirou Touré, UNICEF.

57. Norbert Engel, private communication, March 2, 1985.

58. United Nations Sudano-Sahelian Office, *Action Plan—Sahel* (New York: United Nations, April 1984).

59. "Evaluation of Drought-Related Acute Undernutrition — Mauritania, 1983," *Morbidity and Mortality Weekly Report,* Centers for Disease Control, Vol. 33, Nos. 40 and 45, 1984.

60. *Safe Water and Waste Disposal for Human Health: A Program Guide,* (Washington, D.C.: U.S. Agency for International Development, 1982); *Human Waste Management For Low-Income Settlements* (Bangkok: Environmental Sanitation Information Center, 1983); World Bank, *Poverty and Basic Needs Series,* "Water Supply and Waste Disposal," Washington, D.C., 1983; and John M. Kalbermatten et al., *Appropriate Sanitation Alternatives* (Baltimore: The Johns Hopkins University Press, 1982).

61. William U. Chandler, *Improving World Health: A Least Cost Strategy.*

62. Peter Morgan, Blair Research Laboratory, Harare, Zimbabwe, private communication, April 3, 1985; Peter Morgan, "Blair Research Bulletins for Rural Water Supply and Sanitation," Blair Laboratory, Harare, Zimbabwe, March 1985.

63. Southern African Development Coordination Conference, *SADCC, Agriculture Toward 2000* (Rome: Food and Agriculture Organization, 1984).

64. Edward Girardet, "Afghanistan: No. 1 need is food," *Christian Science Monitor*, December 28, 1984.

65. Institute of Nutrition and Food Science, "Nutrition Survey of Rural Bangladesh"; Mushtag Ahmed and D.J. Clements, "Problems Associated with Wheat Production in Bangladesh," and "Food Policy," editorial in *ADAB News*, September-October 1984; Hugh Brammer, "Development Strategies in Famine Prone Areas," *ADAB News*, November-December 1984.

66. John Burns, "A record grain crop is changing China," *New York Times*, April 2, 1985; Development of Zimbabwe's revolution is described in David Smith and Colin Simpson, *Mugabe* (Harare: Pioneer Head, 1981); Glenn Frankel, "Zimbabwe's Prosperity Depends on Modern Farms, Corn Patches," *Washington Post*, November 20, 1984; Henry Kamm, "Bouyant Zimbabwe Beating Drought," *New York Times*, December 2, 1984; Jan Raath, "Zimbabwe Peasants Reap Huge Harvest," *Christian Science Monitor*, April 17, 1985.

67. World Bank, *World Development Report 1983* (New York: Oxford University Press, 1983); see David K. Willis, "Link Between Aid Terms and Riots in Africa," *Christian Science Monitor*, April 16, 1985, and Jonathan C. Randall, "Sudan Struggling With the Economics of 'There is None,'" *Washington Post*, February 17, 1985.

68. E. A. Ripley, "Drought in the Sahara: Insufficient Biogeophysical Feedback?" *Science*, January 9, 1976; United Nations, *Action Plan—Sahel.*

69. SADCC, *Agriculture Toward 2000.*

70. Ann Crittenden, "Shortchanging a Food Program That Works," *Wall Street Journal*, February 28, 1985; International Fund for Agricultural Development, *A Fund For the Rural Poor* (Rome: IFAD, 1984).

71. Robert Orr Whyte and Pauline Whyte, *The Women of Rural Asia* (Boulder, Colo.: Westview Press, 1982); Edna G. Bay, ed., *Women and Work in Africa* (Boulder, Colo.: Westview Press, 1982); Catherine Overholt et al., eds., *Gender Roles in Development Projects* (West Hartford, Conn.: Kumarian Press, 1985); Karen Oppenheim Mason, *The Status of Women* (New York: The Rockefeller Foundation, 1984); Natalie Kaufman Hevener, *International Law and the Status of Women* (Boulder, Colo.: Westview Press, 1983); U.S. Bureau of the Census and U.S. Agency for International Development, *Women of the World: Sub-Saharan Africa* (Washington, D.C.: U.S. Department of Commerce, 1984); U.S. Bureau of the Census and U.S. Agency for International Development, *Women of the World: Latin America and the Caribbean* (Washington, D.C.: U.S. Department of Commerce, 1984); and Sue Ellen M. Charlton, *Women in Third World Development* (Boulder, Colo.: Westview Press, 1984).

72. National Research Council Board on Science and Technology for International Development, *Agroforestry in the West African Sahel* (Washington, D.C.: National Academy Press, 1983).

73. Hugh O'Haire, "Beyond Family Planning In Indonesia," *Populi*, Vol. 11, No. 3, 1984; David Pyle in *Gender Roles in Development Projects*, Catherine Overholt et al., ed. (West Hartford, Conn.: Kumarian Press, 1985).

74. Maie Ayoub, UNICEF Information Officer, Addis Ababa, Ethiopia, private communication, March 27, 1985; Hans Hurni, Ethiopian Soil Conservation Project, Addis Ababa, Ethiopia, private communication, March 29, 1985.

75. Hans Hurni to Edward C. Wolf, Washington, D.C., private communication, January 9, 1985.

76. M. Padmini, UNICEF Representative, Ethiopia, private communication, March 27, 1985; Hans Hurni, private communication, March 30, 1985.

77. SADCC, *Agriculture Toward 2000; World Development Report 1984*.

78. U.S. Bureau of the Census and U.S. A.I.D., *Women of the World: Sub-Saharan Africa*; U.S. Bureau of the Census and U.S. A.I.D., *Women of the World: Latin America and the Caribbean*; Robert Orr Whyte and Pauline Whyte, *The Women of Rural Asia*; James Trussell and Anne R. Pebley, "The Potential Impact of Changes in Fertility on Infant, Child, and Maternal Mortality," *Studies in Family Planning*, November/December 1984; and Marilyn Edmonds and John M. Paxman, "Early Pregnancy and Childbearing in Guatemala, Brazil, Nigeria, and Indonesia: Addressing the Consequences," *Pathpapers*, Pathfinder Fund, Boston, September 1984.

79. *State of the World's Children 1984;* Cécile de Sweemer, "The Influence of Child Spacing on Child Survival," *Population Studies,* 38, 1984; M. Potts, B.S. Janowitz, and J.A. Forney, eds., *Childbirth In Developing Countries* (Hingham, Mass.: MTP Press, 1983); Rudolfo A. Bulato and Ronald D. Lee, *Determinants of Fertility in Developing Countries,* Vols. 1 and 2 (New York: Academic Press, 1983).

80. John Trussell and Anne R. Pebley, "The Potential Impact of Changes in Fertility on Infant, Child, and Maternal Mortality."

81. World Bank, *World Development Report 1984;* "In Kenya, Modernization, Drop in Breastfeeding and Low Contraceptive Use Bring Rising Fertility," *International Family Planning Perspectives,* Vol. 10, No. 4, 1984; Maleba Gomes, "Family size and education attainment in Kenya," *Population and Development Review,* Vol. 10, No. 4, 1984.

82. Getachew Yoseph and Mekonnen Tadesse, "Present and Projected Population," *Ethiopian Highlands Reclamation Study,* Ministry of Agriculture, Provisional Military Government of the People's Republic of Ethiopia, February 1984; Worldwatch Institute estimates.

83. Nancy Harris, Regional Director, African Region, International Family Planning Assistance, Nairobi, Kenya, private communication, March 26, 1985.

84. Translated by U.S. Department of State, March 1985.

85. United Nations Fund for Population Activities, *1983 Report by the Executive Director* (New York: 1984).

86. Robert Lapham and W. Parker Mauldin, "Family Planning Program Effort and Birthrate Decline in Developing Countries," *International Family Planning Perspectives,* Vol. 10, No. 4, 1984.

87. "Tunisia WFS: Government Family Planning Program Strong; Modern Methods Predominant; But Rural Unmet Need High," *International Family Planning Perspectives,* October 1983; Hugh O'Haire, "Beyond Family Planning in Indonesia"; J.S. Parsons, "Indonesian Family Planning Tick," *Populi,* Vol. 11, No. 3, 1984.

88. Data on life expectancy from World Bank, *World Development Report 1984;* see also, Bulato and Lee, *Determinants of Fertility in Developing Countries; China*

Socialist Economic Development, Vol. III, The Social Sectors: Population, Health, Nutrition, and Education (Washington, D.C.: The World Bank, 1983); Zha Ruichuan, "The Evolution of Fertility in China," State Family Planning Commission, Beijing, People's Republic of China, 1985.

89. Stanley Freed and Ruth Freed, "One Son Is No Sons," *Natural History*, January 1985.

90. J. Knoel et al., *Fertility in Thailand: Trends, Differentials, and Proximate Determinants* (Washington, D.C.: National Academy Press, 1982); and Barbara Entwisle et al., "A Multilevel Model of Family Planning Availability and Contraceptive Use in Rural Thailand," *Demography*, Vol. 21, No. 4, 1984.

91. Linda Harrar, WGBH, Boston, Massachusetts, interview with Mufaweza Khan, Executive Director, Concerned Women's Family Planning Project, Dakha, Bangladesh, private communication, April 1985.

92. Latham and Mauldin, "Family Planning Program Effort and Birthrate Decline in Developing Countries."

93. *Ibid.*; "In Kenya, Modernization, Drop in Breastfeeding and Low Contraceptive Use Bring Rising Fertility," *International Family Planning Perspectives*, Vol. 10, No. 4, 1984; *World Development Report 1984*.

94. David Willis, "Price tag on slowing world population growth: $4 billion a year," *Christian Science Monitor*, August 16, 1984; Joseph Speidel, "Cost Implications of Population Stabilization," presented at the International Workshop on Cost-Effectiveness and Cost-Benefit Analysis in Family Planning Programs, St. Michael's, Maryland, August 17-20, 1981; R. A. Bulatao, draft memorandum to the World Bank, April 9, 1984.

95. Robert Orr Whyte and Pauline Whyte, *The Women of Rural Asia*; Ministry of Community Development and Women's Affairs in cooperation with UNICEF, "Report On The Situation Of Women In Zimbabwe," Harare, Zimbabwe, February 1982.

96. Michael P. Todaro, *Economic Development in the Third World* (London: Langman Group Ltd., 1977); *World Development Report 1983*.

97. These estimates are for illustrative purposes only. Precise calculations would require better data on the population in need as well as the widely variable costs of delivering health care, family planning, education, and agricultural loans. The estimates for health care and sanitation are extra-

polated from case studies and estimates found in the literature as detailed in Chandler, *Improving World Health: A Least Cost Strategy*. The incremental cost of extending family planning to unserved people includes an assumption of rapid fertility decline amounting to a linear decrease of .216 percent per year until equilibrium is reached. The estimate was made by Speidel, "Cost Implications of Population Stabilization," and Bulatao, draft memorandum to the World Bank. The cost of education per pupil is derived from *World Development Report 1984*. The cost of providing agricultural productivity loans is a crude extrapolation from the experience of the International Fund for Agricultural Development (See IFAD, *A Fund for the Rural Poor*), and experience in Zimbabwe. Most estimates include a conservative assumption that the high end of the range of costs will be necessary for delivery of the services.

98. Organisation for Economic Cooperation and Development, *Development Cooperation* (Paris: 1984).

WILLIAM U. CHANDLER is a Senior Researcher at Worldwatch Institute in Washington, D.C. He is author of Worldwatch Paper 59, *Improving World Health: A Least Cost Strategy*, and *The Myth of TVA*, as well as many articles on energy and the environment.

THE WORLDWATCH PAPER SERIES

No. of
Copies

1. **The Other Energy Crisis: Firewood** by Erik Eckholm.
2. **The Politics and Responsibility of the North American Breadbasket** by Lester R. Brown.
3. **Women in Politics: A Global Review** by Kathleen Newland.
4. **Energy: The Case for Conservation** by Denis Hayes.
5. **Twenty-two Dimensions of the Population Problem** by Lester R. Brown, Patricia L. McGrath, and Bruce Stokes.
6. **Nuclear Power: The Fifth Horseman** by Denis Hayes.
7. **The Unfinished Assignment: Equal Education for Women** by Patricia L. McGrath.
8. **World Population Trends: Signs of Hope, Signs of Stress** by Lester R. Brown.
9. **The Two Faces of Malnutrition** by Erik Eckholm and Frank Record.
10. **Health: The Family Planning Factor** by Erik Eckholm and Kathleen Newland.
11. **Energy: The Solar Prospect** by Denis Hayes.
12. **Filling The Family Planning Gap** by Bruce Stokes.
13. **Spreading Deserts—The Hand of Man** by Erik Eckholm and Lester R. Brown.
14. **Redefining National Security** by Lester R. Brown.
15. **Energy for Development: Third World Options** by Denis Hayes.
16. **Women and Population Growth: Choice Beyond Childbearing** by Kathleen Newland.
17. **Local Responses to Global Problems: A Key to Meeting Basic Human Needs** by Bruce Stokes.
18. **Cutting Tobacco's Toll** by Erik Eckholm.
19. **The Solar Energy Timetable** by Denis Hayes.
20. **The Global Economic Prospect: New Sources of Economic Stress** by Lester R. Brown.
21. **Soft Technologies, Hard Choices** by Colin Norman.
22. **Disappearing Species: The Social Challenge** by Erik Eckholm.
23. **Repairs, Reuse, Recycling—First Steps Toward a Sustainable Society** by Denis Hayes.
24. **The Worldwide Loss of Cropland** by Lester R. Brown.
25. **Worker Participation—Productivity and the Quality of Work Life** by Bruce Stokes.
26. **Planting for the Future: Forestry for Human Needs** by Erik Eckholm.
27. **Pollution: The Neglected Dimensions** by Denis Hayes.
28. **Global Employment and Economic Justice: The Policy Challenge** by Kathleen Newland.
29. **Resource Trends and Population Policy: A Time for Reassessment** by Lester R. Brown.
30. **The Dispossessed of the Earth: Land Reform and Sustainable Development** by Erik Eckholm.
31. **Knowledge and Power: The Global Research and Development Budget** by Colin Norman.
32. **The Future of the Automobile in an Oil-Short World** by Lester R. Brown, Christopher Flavin, and Colin Norman.
33. **International Migration: The Search for Work** by Kathleen Newland.
34. **Inflation: The Rising Cost of Living on a Small Planet** by Robert Fuller.
35. **Food or Fuel: New Competition for the World's Cropland** by Lester R. Brown.
36. **The Future of Synthetic Materials: The Petroleum Connection** by Christopher Flavin.
37. **Women, Men, and The Division of Labor** by Kathleen Newland.
38. **City Limits: Emerging Constraints on Urban Growth** by Kathleen Newland.

_____ 39. **Microelectronics at Work: Productivity and Jobs in the World Economy** by Colin Norman.
_____ 40. **Energy and Architecture: The Solar and Conservation Potential** by Christopher Flavin.
_____ 41. **Men and Family Planning** by Bruce Stokes.
_____ 42. **Wood: An Ancient Fuel with a New Future** by Nigel Smith.
_____ 43. **Refugees: The New International Politics of Displacement** by Kathleen Newland.
_____ 44. **Rivers of Energy: The Hydropower Potential** by Daniel Deudney.
_____ 45. **Wind Power: A Turning Point** by Christopher Flavin.
_____ 46. **Global Housing Prospects: The Resource Constraints** by Bruce Stokes.
_____ 47. **Infant Mortality and the Health of Societies** by Kathleen Newland.
_____ 48. **Six Steps to a Sustainable Society** by Lester R. Brown and Pamela Shaw.
_____ 49. **Productivity: The New Economic Context** by Kathleen Newland.
_____ 50. **Space: The High Frontier in Perspective** by Daniel Deudney.
_____ 51. **U.S. and Soviet Agriculture: The Shifting Balance of Power** by Lester R. Brown.
_____ 52. **Electricity from Sunlight: The Future of Photovoltaics** by Christopher Flavin.
_____ 53. **Population Policies for a New Economic Era** by Lester R. Brown.
_____ 54. **Promoting Population Stabilization: Incentives for Small Families** by Judith Jacobsen.
_____ 55. **Whole Earth Security: A Geopolitics of Peace** by Daniel Deudney
_____ 56. **Materials Recycling: The Virtue of Necessity** by William U. Chandler.
_____ 57. **Nuclear Power: The Market Test** by Christopher Flavin
_____ 58. **Air Pollution, Acid Rain, and the Future of Forests** by Sandra Postel
_____ 59. **Improving World Health: A Least Cost Strategy** by William U. Chandler
_____ 60. **Soil Erosion: Quiet Crisis in the World Economy** by Lester Brown and Edward Wolf.
_____ 61. **Electricity's Future: The Shift to Efficiency and Small-Scale Power** by Christopher Flavin
_____ 62. **Water: Rethinking Management in an Age of Scarcity** by Sandra Postel
_____ 63. **Energy Productivity: Key to Environmental Protection and Economic Progress** by William U. Chandler
_____ 64. **Investing in Children** by William U. Chandler

_____ Total Copies

Single Copy—$4.00

Bulk Copies (any combination of titles)
2-5: $3.00 each   5-20: $2.00 each   21 or more: $1.00 each

Calendar Year Subscription (1985 subscription begins with Paper 63)
U.S. $25.00 _____

Make check payable to Worldwatch Institute
1776 Massachusetts Avenue NW, Washington, D.C. 20036 USA

Enclosed is my check for U.S. $ _____

name

address

city   state   zip/country